THE CALL

Leading from Wholeness,
Living in Presence

EMMANUEL ADESEKO

The Call
Leading from Wholeness, Living in Presence

The Call Framework Diagram courtesy of Sarah Yetunde.

ISBN: 978-1-918038-74-3

Contents

Endorsements

'God prepares every vessel He uses. The process is not pleasant yet necessary. He orchestrates situations and events to break us again and again until we are broken and malleable in His hands. Only then is a vessel fit for divine purpose. Apostle Adeseko has succinctly chronicled this divine process in his book. He opens himself up and paints for his readers a mosaic of this divine process on the canvass of his life. As a master craftsman, he draws us into his encounters with pain, successes, failures, and his triumphs. We see God's work of restoration in his life and the unfolding of divine purpose. Son, you are a vessel plucked from fire. Keep soaring!'

Dr Ralph Dartey
General Overseer of Transforming Life Centre International

'I first met Emmanuel many years ago—he was just 16, and I was 15. What immediately bonded us was the fire of God that had touched our lives. We had encountered His presence, devoted ourselves to prayer, and immersed deeply in His Word. As I turned the pages of this book, my eyes welled with tears, reflecting on Emmanuel's journey. I have witnessed him passionately pursue God, mature in his Apostolic and teaching ministry, step into his calling in business, and mentor countless others—even while enduring intense battles and trials that could have easily overwhelmed him. What makes this book extraordinary is that it is not merely words on paper, but a living testimony of victory through God's grace. Emmanuel has transformed seasons of pain and brokenness into a powerful life manual that inspires, challenges, and equips believers to step into the fullness of God's plan. Within these pages, you will gain fresh strength and develop a warrior's mindset—one that empowers you to walk boldly in your calling and fulfil everything God has designed you to BE and to DO for His glory. Open your heart, dive in, and be encouraged!'

Pastor Tim Adelegan
Founder of Glory Church & Prayer Army Network

'I highly recommend this book. Apostle Emmanuel is a gifted orator, and voice to the Nations. He marries prophetic clarity and apostolic wisdom with such grace. This book is an extension of the wisdom God has given him and is a clear message of hope! '

Dr Kofi Dartey
Founder of Campus Rush Global & Minstrel Records

'I highly recommend this book to every believer—especially those called to lead. I know Apostle Emmanuel Adeseko personally. He is a dear brother and friend of mine, and one of the most prolific teachers of the Word I know. His depth of insight, coupled with a genuine heart for truth and restoration, shines through every page of this book. What makes this work so unique is its raw honesty. Apostle Emmanuel does not write from theory or distance—he writes from the trenches of real life, where grace met brokenness. In a world where many hide behind platforms and polished images, this book is refreshingly different. It does not present make-up; it reveals scars—and in doing so, it reflects the very nature of Christ. When Jesus appeared to Thomas after His resurrection, He didn't hide His scars. He showed them. He allowed His wounds to become the very proof of His identity and victory. That moment brought not only healing but conviction. In the same way, the vulnerability in this book carries the power to heal, awaken, and realign those who are silently struggling under the weight of leadership and calling. Apostle Emmanuel's journey—marked by repentance, restoration, and revelation—will be a lifeline for many. This is more than a book. It is a divine tool for inner healing, spiritual recalibration, and a deeper walk with God. I wholeheartedly commend it to you. Read it with an open heart. It will bless you deeply.'

Pastor Randolph Adjei
Founder of Kingdom Ambassadors Centre & Upper Room Global Prayer Movement

"In John 20:27, our Lord Jesus uses His wounds as proof of His resurrection to a doubting disciple. In a time when perfection, innovation, and image define success—especially in ministry—it is rare to find a leader who humbly acknowledges past mistakes. But from such ashes often rises a more refined servant, sharpened as an arrow for the Kingdom, ready to confront the enemy at the gate. Apostle Emmanuel Adeseko's journey is a sobering and powerful reflection. Within these pages, we encounter brokenness, honesty, accountability, and responsibility—the true marks of a child of God and an effective leader. I wholeheartedly recommend this book to current and emerging leaders. It is a timely tool to equip Kingdom functionaries. I can only thank God for your life—a true soldier of Christ."

Pastor Mani Witenkate
Senior Pastor of Transformation Church & Founder of Ruach Ireland Ministry

Foreword

Apostle Emmanuel, I have known for over 10 years. I have known him through his heights of ministry, with great testimonies of the miraculous. But I have also known him through his lows, where he has sought God for greater transformation into God's image. I have a term that I use, and I've preached over the years. It's called leading while bleeding. So many young leaders fall into this category, but Emmanuel is one of those that has come through it with a right attitude, with correct motives, and with the anointing and the peace of God upon his life. In this age there's many leaders that speak from success, but this book dares to speak from surrender, which offers a blueprint to many. Not from a pedestal position, but also from the valley position. I think you will gain out of this book a desire for godly boundaries, a greater sense of protection from God the Father, the ability to walk in vulnerability without being weak. The ability to navigate your paradigm with the Holy Spirit. As I read this book, I can attest to its timely and prophetic messages to all, especially leaders across many different contexts.

So, I want to recommend this book. I also want to affirm the credibility of its message and the integrity of its author. Emmanuel's Journey can help take you through a process that is authentic for growth and commissioning to your high call. God has truly given him a message for this generation.

Dr Sharon Stone
Founder of Prophetic Voice

Preface: You Are Crazy!

You are crazy! That's what I would tell you. If you told me that I would one day step down from pastoring the ministry I had founded, I would've thought something is wrong with you. Yet within a single day, I resigned from a ministry I had led for several years and saw a significant personal relationship come to an end. It was disorienting and painful.

Looking back, I realised that my journey into this season was not due to one single event, but a culmination of years of compounded loss, pressure and trauma. In previous years, I had experienced heartbreak in a relationship and the loss of a dear friend and brother in the church I pastored. I had the honour to assist in planning and coordinating the funeral with his wife and family, but it was unbelievably difficult as I was also grieving, heartbroken, and leading a church through its own period of grief. Like many leaders, I kept going—believing that perseverance alone could carry me through. But back then, what I thought was resilience was, in some ways, self-abandonment and avoidance of the deeper restoration I needed. At first, I thought: 'That situation was tough! but I fought through it and kept going. Surely, I can do the same now?'.

It's a common belief most leaders have: just push through and keep going. That's true in some instances, however in this instance it was not the time to 'just keep going'. I must admit this wasn't easy. I feared people would think I'd done something unspeakable if I stayed away too long. However, this time, through the counsel of trusted voices, including my spiritual mother Dr. Sharon, I made a decision that was counter to my instincts: I stopped everything. Have you ever found yourself rescuing others while silently needing rescue yourself? That was me. Leading while bleeding.

Showing up for everyone else while quietly falling apart. But the truth is, I couldn't even identify where I was bleeding. I just knew back then that something was broken within me. This time however, no more rescuing others. I needed to allow Jesus to rescue me. It wasn't that I was being malicious to anyone or intentionally neglectful of myself. In fact, I had therapy before for a short season. However, the sheer weight of responsibility had become a distraction from the deeper healing I truly needed. I cancelled all public ministry for a year, creating space to address what I now know was the underlying cause—a mix of unprocessed grief, ministry strain, and personal brokenness. I came face to face with these compounded traumas – years of ministry strain, unresolved pain including revisiting the grief of losing my father, the shock of hearing of my cousin's murder and the hidden wounds from being molested as a child. These weren't just past events—they were deeply formative experiences that shaped how I coped, how I led, and how I related to God, myself and others. I also needed to acknowledge that I made poor choices at times that caused hurt to myself and others, and patterns that were no longer sustainable. That year became a turning point. I entered intentional restoration—therapy, accountability, repentance, prayer, fasting and allowing God to bring light into the parts of my story that had remained wounded and unattended for too long.

During that time, I truly learnt what the word 'despair' meant. At times I had sleepless nights, lack of appetite, fear, shame, regret, embarrassment, injustice, betrayal, anger, confusion, condemnation: you name it I felt it. Have you ever wanted to pray but have felt too heavy to open your mouth and didn't even know what to say? Well, at times that was me. There were days when prayer felt impossible and hope seemed far away. But early on I had one encounter with the Holy Spirit that changed everything—reminding me that my sending and calling were not revoked. This experience - marked with the tangible presence of God - released an impartation that brought grace to pray and inspired great hope for the future. While I won't share every detail here, I can say this: the process was a painful, stretching, and ultimately life-transforming journey of prayer, therapy, repentance, healing and restoration. Now I can say it's one of the best things God has done for me!

A year later, I can say with confidence: I am healed from the fractures in my heart that caused me to bleed. No more leaking. No more false identities. No more compounded trauma. Clarity in God's call for my life. Rooted in deep, unshakable intimacy with Christ. This isn't just healing—it's wholeness.

'For you, O God, have tested us; you have tried us as silver is tried. You brought us into the net; you laid a crushing burden on our backs; you let men ride over our heads; we went through fire and through water; yet you have brought us out to a place of abundance.' – Psalm 66:10-12

God has given me a word—and I write this book with strong conviction and fire in my bones, as both a testimony and a divine guide for pastors, leaders, and anyone who hungers to discover and walk boldly in the calling of God – whatever context you're in. This is for those who refuse to settle for surface-level faith, false identities and desire instead to lead, live, and serve from a place of deep intimacy with Christ, emotional and spiritual wholeness, walk in power and a holy reverence for His presence.

What God has done in me, and through me, has turned my life upside down. It's transformed the way I live, the way I relate to God, the way I lead, the way I minister, and the way I carry His name. He has brought me out of a shaped by the Spirit's ongoing work and expressed in the life of the church (then to the world).

This book is built on that conviction. It offers a practical theology of leadership that is deeply rooted in the Gospel and applicable to any context. Your leadership is not separate from your discipleship—*it is the fruit of it.*

In addition to offering a theological framework, this book also shares a testimony of how the Holy Spirit has worked through real-life situations, often in unexpected and refining ways. It is both theological and personal—demonstrating how God shapes leaders through grace, truth, and experience.

This book will offer teaching, practical application, prophetic insight, and sound theology—but it will also include *me*. I am not writing from a distance; I am writing from within the journey. In many ways, *I am the book, and the book is me.*

In my earlier years of ministry, I was more comfortable being known for the *work* I did than for *who* I was. I didn't realise how much I was contributing to being misunderstood—and, at times, to living in a way that lacked authenticity. But I've come to realise that sharing my own story is not a distraction from truth—it's part of how truth becomes real and relatable. The principles in this book are not just wrapped in theological language—they've been lived, tested, and proven in the fire of real life and ministry.

Let me be honest—I've deleted and rewritten some parts of this book 30 times, thinking, *"Nah, I can't say that!"* But I've learned that vulnerability is part of leadership. So, I've chosen to be as real as I can, even when it's uncomfortable, because I believe the most powerful truth is the one we live, not just the one we preach.

I want to be clear: I have *not* arrived. I'm still growing. But I've come through a process—refined, healed, transformed and made whole by the grace of God. And because of that, I now speak with the authority and right that comes from testimony, not just theory. What I share here isn't borrowed knowledge; it's hard-won truth.

I've done my best to keep it honest and real, because I want you to see more than just teaching—I want you to encounter something of Jesus for yourself. This is not something I just Googled or copied; it's what I've lived, and I can testify that it's real and life-changing when applied. Testimony is powerful. As Revelation 12:11 reminds us, *"They overcame him by the blood of the Lamb and by the word of their testimony."* My prayer is that as I share mine, you'll be encouraged and empowered to find victory in your own journey too.

I will summarise my convictions in a thesis statement: This book contends that equipping leaders for holistic transformation is essential to empowering them to overcome personal obstacles, cultivate deep intimacy with Christ, discern their divine calling, lead from a place of wholeness, steward their mission with integrity, carry Gods presence and become catalysts for lasting impact in their families, teams, ministries, organisations and the world.

Who is this book for?

This book is a divine guide for pastors, leaders, and anyone who hungers to discover and walk boldly in the calling of God—regardless of the context you find yourself in. Some of you may be reading this while in a place of deep discouragement. You've lost hope and are stuck in a situation you never imagined you'd be in. You're searching for a way out—or perhaps even considering giving up altogether. Others are wounded from life and ministry—still leading, but silently bleeding—barely functioning under the weight of it all. And some of you are emerging or aspiring leaders, eager to discern your calling and seeking the wisdom to steward it well. Some of you are seasoned leaders. Wherever you're coming from—whether broken, burdened, or simply longing for more—if you open your heart and mind, this book will meet you there.

It is written for those who desire to grow in the fear of God and carry His presence with integrity and courage. This book carries a prophetic assignment: to redeem lost identities, restore the broken, equip leaders, and call the Church to repentance. The restoration I've experienced wasn't just for me—through it, Christ gave me a message for His people (Luke 22:32). I believe the truths revealed through my journey of realignment, repentance and healing can and will transform the lives of all who are willing to receive it.

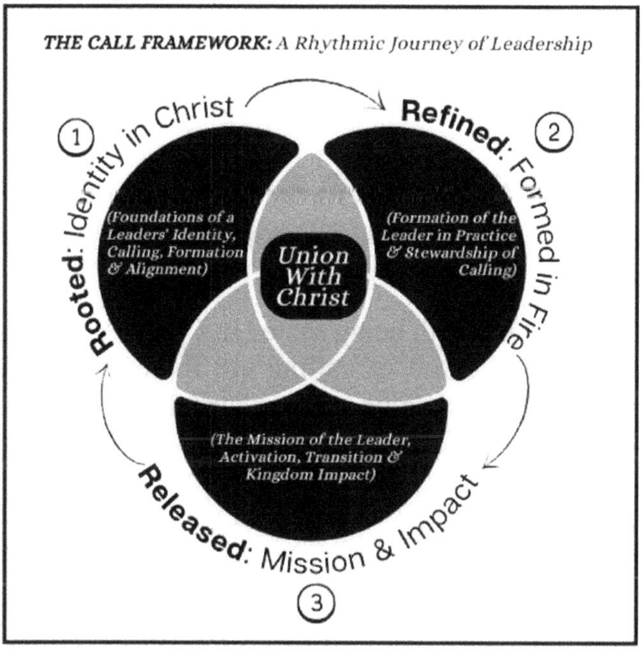

I, Emmanuel Adeseko, developed *The Call Framework* to capture the rhythmic journey of a leader's development. The framework identifies three interconnected dimensions—**Rooted, Refined, and Released**—that together describe both the inner and outer life of a leader. To be **Rooted** is to anchor one's identity and calling in Christ, building on the unshakable foundation of intimacy and alignment with Him. To be **Refined** is to embrace the challenges, conflicts, and tests that shape character, strengthen resilience and equip the leader to steward their calling. To be **Released** is to step into Kingdom assignment, living out God's mission with authority and impact. These are not linear stages to be ticked off, but a sacred rhythm: roots (identity in Christ) feed the refining, refining (formation in practice) empowers the release

The Rhythm of Leadership

The arrows show that leadership is not linear, but cyclical. Foundations flow into formation, formation fuels mission, and mission circles back—testing and deepening both the formation and foundation of the leader. This rhythm never ends, but it is more than a cycle but iterative. This means repetition with progressive improvement — each round build on the previous one. Not necessarily returning to the exact start; instead, refining, developing and evolving. In scripture we understand this progression as going "from glory to glory" (2 Corinthians 3:18). However, the diagram advises leaders to begin at Section 1: Identity in Christ. Without this starting point, leaders risk entering formation in practice or mission unprepared, which leads to burnout, compromise, or misalignment. Union with Christ at the centre is the anchor—holding together identity, formation, and mission in balance and wholeness.

So, as you read this book, do so prayerfully and with open hands. This isn't just theory—it's testimony, it's warning, it's impartation, and it's an invitation. May God give you grace, wisdom, and courage to rise into the kind of leader He is raising for this hour.

We need you. The Kingdom needs you. The future demands it. The next generation needs it.

Let's Pray: 'Father, as I open this book, I invite You to invade every area of my life—even the places I'm unaware need Your touch. Reach deep within me. Transform me. Shape me into a better man, woman, pastor, husband, wife, businessman, prophet, and leader. As I read, let Your Spirit align my heart with You, with myself, and with others in ways I've never experienced before. Let this be more than information—let it be a divine encounter that changes me from the inside out. In Jesus' name, Amen.'

Section 1 - Rooted: Identity in Christ

Foundations of a Leaders' *Identity, Calling, Formation & Alignment*

Focus: Calling, formation, identity, process and early wounds that shape leadership.

Chapter 1

The Blueprint: Understanding Your Kingdom Assignment

Blueprint Moments: A Personal Reflection

As I wrestled with what it truly meant to walk in my Kingdom assignment, I found myself having repeated conversations with Dr. Sharon—each one peeling back layers of insight and identity. In one of those pivotal sessions, she looked at me with clarity and conviction and said: "It's about the Kingdom of God and Jesus." That simple statement reoriented my focus. She explained that if I were to understand and steward my assignment well, I had to start with God's mission as the blueprint. "From that place," she said, "you'll know what to say yes to—and how to measure impact that actually matters in eternity." What impacted me most was her uncompromising stance on holiness. "Find the testimony in this process, Emmanuel," she told me. "The very area the enemy tried to bring destruction is the very place where God will gain the glory. But to be entrusted with the high call of God on your life, you must allow Him to cultivate holiness—not just as abstinence, but as a moment-by-moment communion with Him, where you know His presence and sense when He is grieved." She often shared real-life examples of how the Holy Spirit had invited her into deeper levels of consecration—not because she was living in sin, but because her assignment carried weight that required greater sensitivity to His presence and responsibility in her calling. What stood out to me was that this wasn't about legalism or fear—it was about love, intimacy, and alignment with God's heart. The closer she walked with Him, the more refined her life became. That stirred something in me:

consecration is not merely about avoiding what is wrong—it's about being fully available for what is right, for what is holy in order to steward what is Kingdom. Your Kingdom assignment demands a life shaped by God's presence, not just His principles. If we want to carry Kingdom authority, we must walk in Kingdom alignment. Dr. Sharon helped me understand: Your assignment isn't just about what you do for God—it's about becoming the kind of person God can trust with His purposes.

Every Christian leader is called to embody and advance the mission of Christ. Though the calling precedes qualification, God faithfully equips those He calls. Regardless of your leadership context—whether in the church, marketplace, or broader community—you must first grasp God's overarching mission and the Church's missional identity. Only from this foundation will you gain the conviction needed in Christ to abandon sin, overcome personal trauma, discern God's calling, and steward it with holy resolve and spiritual authority. That's the focus of this chapter. I want you to see how God's covenantal relationship with Abraham reveals that His mission, our election, and godliness are inseparable—together forming the theological foundation and driving force behind Christian leadership and participating in Christ's mission on earth today.

Genesis 18:16-21 states: ' '*Then the men set out from there, and they looked down toward Sodom. And Abraham went with them to set them on their way. The Lord said, "Shall I hide from Abraham what I am about to do, seeing that Abraham shall surely become a great and mighty nation, and all the nations of the earth shall be blessed in him? For I have chosen him, that he may command his children and his household after him to keep the way of the Lord by doing righteousness and justice, so that the Lord may bring to*

Abraham what he has promised him." Then the Lord said, "Because the outcry against Sodom and Gomorrah is great and their sin is very grave, I will go down to see whether they have done altogether according to the outcry that has come to me. And if not, I will know."

Historical Context of Genesis

Genesis, the first book of the Bible, offers more than just the origins of the world and the people of Israel—it provides foundational revelations about God's nature, His purposes, and His relationship with humanity. The book is traditionally divided into two major parts: the primaeval history (Genesis 1–11), which traces the creation, the fall, and the spread of humanity and the patriarchal history (Genesis 12–50), which focuses on the lives of Israel's ancestors, beginning with Abraham. Moses is widely regarded as the traditional author.

Chapters 18 and 19 form a deeply theological and unified narrative. The Lord appears to Abraham at Mamre (18:1–15), invites him into divine dialogue through intercession for Sodom (18:16–33), and ultimately delivers Lot while executing righteous judgement (19:1–29). These are not just historical moments—they are prophetic windows into how God invites His people to participate in His redemptive mission. What unfolds in Abraham's encounter with God is more than a personal calling—it is a revelation of God's heart for the world and a blueprint for how chosen people are to live. In these chapters, we see three themes emerge with striking clarity: God's mission to bless the nations, the election of Abraham to be a vessel of that mission, and the call to godliness as the only way the promise is to be fulfilled.

For Christian leaders today, this narrative is not just informative—it is formative. It challenges us to see leadership as covenantal responsibility, not personal status. It shows that our election is not an end in itself, but a call to righteous influence for the sake of others. It emphasises that godliness is not private piety but active alignment with God's justice and righteousness to fulfil His mission. In the next section, I will unpack these three interconnected themes—God's mission, our election and godliness—and explore how they shape our identity, leadership, and participation in God's kingdom assignment on earth.

1. The Mission of God: Blessing the Nations

Genesis 18:17–19 marks a moment of profound divine self-disclosure. As the Lord contemplates the judgement of Sodom, He invites Abraham into the conversation—not out of obligation, but because of purpose. God says, "Shall I hide from Abraham what I am about to do…?" Why? Because Abraham has been chosen to be more than a passive recipient of God's blessing; he is to be an active agent of it. God's mission, revealed here, is to bless the nations through Abraham. But what does it mean to "bless the nations"? The Hebrew word for "bless" (barak) carries rich meaning— "to kneel," "to empower," "to bestow benefit." In Genesis, blessing signifies divine enablement—a release of God's favour, resources, and reward to empower people to live according to His creational design (Genesis 1:26). In Genesis 12:1–3, this blessing includes a great name, a multitude of descendants, and—most crucially—the promise that "all the nations of the earth shall be blessed" through Abraham.

The Apostle Paul later describes this blessing as the Gospel itself (Gal. 3:8), fulfilled ultimately in Jesus Christ, the seed of Abraham (Gal. 3:16). Therefore, those who belong to Christ are not only recipients of Abraham's blessing (Rom. 4; Gal. 3), but also participants in Abraham's mission. In other words: if you are in Christ, you carry Abraham's global assignment. Whatever your context—ministry, business, fashion, real estate, government, education—this assignment does not require you to hold a microphone or stand behind a pulpit. Even if you're not directly preaching the gospel, your life will still carry two inseparable dimensions:

- <u>Evangelistic Dimension:</u> Your lifestyle is a witness—a living demonstration of what it looks like to live under God's creational design and blessing marked by justice, righteousness, peace, integrity, and fruitfulness.
- <u>Evangelistic Intention:</u> Through proclamation of God's word and demonstration, you are called to directly invite others to repentance and faith in Jesus for eternal life, and to enter this redemptive reality themselves.

This is the essence of being blessed to be a blessing: your whole life becomes an embodiment of God's mission—wherever He has placed you.

<u>Sodom: A Prophetic Model</u>

This divine conversation between God and Abraham doesn't happen in isolation. It's set against the backdrop of the impending judgement of Sodom—a city so corrupt that its cry of injustice has risen to Heaven. The Hebrew word used here for "outcry" (zeaqah) means a scream of pain or distress. It's the same word used in Exodus 2:23 when the Israelites groaned under Egyptian slavery. Just as God responded then, He responds now—because His mission includes confronting evil, rescuing the oppressed, and establishing righteousness. The word Sodom, used 39 times in the Old Testament, means “scorched” or “burned.” It has become symbolic of moral collapse, injustice, and divine judgement. The city's legacy of sexual perversion and gross inhospitality (Gen. 19:1–11) makes it a biblical type of fallen humanity – the world we are in today. The prophets and apostles refer to Sodom to warn God’s people of societal decay (e.g., Deut. 29:16–28; Isa. 1:9–11; Amos 4:11; Rom. 9:29; Matt. 10:15). What’s striking in Genesis 18 is that God reveals His global redemptive purpose (to bless nations) in the same breath as His local act of judgement (against Sodom). The theological implication is clear: God’s mission is not merely about blessing individuals or nations—it’s about restoring justice, confronting sin, and drawing humanity into alignment with His kingdom. Sodom is local, but God’s mission is global. While the narrative centres on a particular city, its implications stretch far beyond geography. Sodom becomes a prophetic metaphor—not only for the fallen world around us, but also for the rebellious tendencies within us. It represents the moral decay, idolatry, and injustice that defy God’s reign, whether in society or in the hidden corners of our own hearts. In this sense, the story challenges us to see that what God confronts in the local—whether in a city, a culture, or an individual—always carries weight in the global and cosmic scope of His mission. The internal must come into alignment with the eternal. For leaders especially, this means we cannot separate personal godliness from global purpose. What we confront locally will have an impact globally. The transformation of the world begins with our willingness to let God confront and redeem the "Sodom" within.

This moment with Abraham shows us the scope of God’s heart: He hears the cries of the oppressed, He judges wickedness, and He empowers His covenant partners to participate in both intercession and mission. The mission of God is holistic. It is both restorative and righteous. And it requires leaders—like Abraham and like us—who will not merely enjoy God's promises but carry God's purpose into the world.

2. Election and Calling

Genesis 18:19 is a theologically profound verse, revealing how God's promise, election, and expectation unite in the life of Abraham. The Lord says, "For I have chosen him" (ESV), or more literally, "I have known him" (NKJV). The Hebrew word used here is 'yaḏah', which means "to know"—not in a casual sense, but in the deepest relational sense. It is the same word used in Genesis 4:1 to describe the union of Adam and Eve, indicating an intimate, covenantal relationship. This sheds crucial light on the nature of election and calling. God's choice of Abraham was not detached from His global mission (v.18)—it was for that mission. God chose Abraham so that through him, all nations might be blessed. Election here is not about favouritism or exclusion; it is about purposeful selection for global impact.

For centuries, debates around election have centred on salvation—whether God predestines some for salvation and not others. But as some scholars (Wright, 2010) rightly argue, this narrow view misses the wider biblical narrative. The context of Genesis 18 shows us that election is best understood as a mission doctrine. God did not choose Abraham instead of the nations; He chose Abraham for the benefit of other nations. Likewise, in Christ, we must embrace this same posture—our election is not a badge of exclusivity, but a call into intimate relationship (yadah) with God for the sake of others. We are set apart not for

righteousness from God's perspective? I would even go so far as to say that justice without righteousness—or righteousness without justice—is often demonic in nature. Why? Because God's throne is founded on both righteousness and justice (Psalm 89:14). This is how He governs the universe and how He intends His people to reflect His rule.

Abraham was commanded to teach his household to walk in the way of the Lord—marked by righteousness and justice. I am convinced that only godly, whole men and women can rightly administer these kingdom values in a world (and Church) desperate for them. This is precisely why the enemy targets families, identity, and wholeness—because he knows broken people cannot fully embody or steward God's justice and righteousness. But no more! It's time for leaders to rise who live healed, lead holy, and govern in truth—leaders who, like Abraham, embody God's heart in both their homes and their callings.

Final Thought

Just as Abraham was chosen to walk closely with God and represent His purposes near the brokenness of Sodom, so too is the Church—God's covenant people—called to embody His righteousness and justice in a fallen world. This calling is not confined to pulpits or religious spaces; it applies to leaders in every sphere—church, marketplace, and community. The greatest threat to the Church's influence is not external opposition, but internal compromise. When we disconnect our identity from God's mission and separate our calling from godliness, we dilute our witness and disqualify ourselves from effective participation in God's redemptive plan. God's election of Abraham was never about exclusion—it was about mission. He was chosen for the benefit of the nations, not their neglect. And if we are in Christ, we too are part of Abraham's household—called not only to receive blessing but to become a channel of it. That means our leadership must be rooted in an intimate relationship with God, shaped by righteousness and justice, and positioned toward the transformation of the world around us. Our obedience matters. Our lives—whether in ministry, business, education, fashion, real estate, or government—must reflect the divine pattern of blessing, justice and righteousness. We are not merely chosen to have God's promises, but to carry His purposes. In this way, mission, election, and godliness are not separate theological ideas, but a singular calling for those who lead in the name of Christ. But here's the tension: you cannot walk in your calling without walking the road of transformation. Righteousness and justice must not only flow from your platform but take root in your character. Your healing, your wholeness, your willingness to let God deal with the Sodom in your own soul—these are not side issues; they are central. Because your authority in the world will never exceed your surrender before God.

So go all in. Take your formation seriously. Take your calling seriously. The world is waiting. And God has entrusted you with a part of His mission that no one else can fulfil in the way He's designed you to. This is your Abrahamic moment. Say yes—not just to the promise, but to the process. Say yes to righteousness, yes to justice, yes to becoming the kind of person through whom God can shape history. Let your leadership be your witness. Let your wholeness be your warfare. Let your life tell the world what it looks like to live under the blessing of God. Only when we truly understand this can we be hungry enough to confront and overcome personal trauma, discern our calling with clarity, and lead with holy resolve and spiritual authority in Christ.

Chapter 1 Reflections – The Blueprint: Understanding Your Kingdom Assignment

Memory Verse

"For I have chosen him, that he may command his children and his household after him to keep the way of the Lord by doing righteousness and justice, so that the Lord may bring to Abraham what he has promised him." — Genesis 18:19

Personal Reflection Questions

1. Understanding God's Mission:
    - Do I truly understand the overarching mission of God to bless the nations? In what ways have I viewed my faith as personal privilege rather than global purpose?
2. Missional Identity:
    - How does seeing election as a missional calling (not just salvation) reshape the way I view my life, work, and leadership?
3. Intimacy with God (Yadah):
    - Am I cultivating an intimate, obedient relationship with God that qualifies me to carry His purposes in the world?
4. Righteousness & Justice:
    - In what areas of my life, family, or leadership am I embodying—or neglecting—righteousness and justice?

5. Godliness & Wholeness:

- Are there areas in my life (personal, emotional, relational) where I need healing or wholeness in order to fully steward my calling?

6. Living Under God's Blessing:

- How does my life demonstrate what it means to live under God's intended creational design? What would others learn about God's ways by observing how I live?

7. Discerning My Assignment:

- Have I taken time to seriously seek God for my specific calling in this season? What distractions or fears keep me from saying "yes" fully?

8. Family & Influence:

- Am I discipling and influencing those around me—family, church, colleagues—toward godliness and mission? What intentional steps can I take?

9. Courage to Lead:

- What would it look like for me to go "all in" on the journey of wholeness, transformation, and calling?

10. Responsibility of Election:

- Do I recognise that my disobedience doesn't just affect me—it impacts the world around me? How seriously am I taking that responsibility?

Closing Prayer

Father, thank You for calling me into Your covenant purpose through Christ Jesus—to walk in intimacy with You, to embody righteousness and justice, and to be a blessing to the world around me. Help me not to take lightly the weight of this calling. Heal what is broken in me. Awaken me to my divine assignment. Empower me to walk in obedience, to disciple those in my sphere, and to reflect Your ways in every area of my life. I say yes—not just to the promise, but to the process. Use me as an instrument of Your mission in my generation. Amen.

Chapter 2

'You Are Not Alone': Held by The Holy Spirit

You are not truly alone. That is the truth at the heart of this chapter. As a Christian leader, you may often carry weight that no one else sees, face pressures that isolate you, and wrestle with pain you can't always explain. But even in those moments, you are never alone—because the Holy Spirit is with you. More than a comforting presence, He is an active partner. If you are willing to participate with Him, the Holy Spirit will faithfully and powerfully guide you through healing, into wholeness, and toward transformation. He knows the depths of who you are, and He leads you not only into what you are called to do, but into who you are becoming.

This chapter will show you how you can participate with the Holy Spirit—specifically as He leads you through healing, wholeness, and growth. Even in your deepest pain or confusion, He is present, speaking, and guiding you into transformation. You are never truly alone. Leadership often demands strength, resilience, and the ability to carry others even when you're barely holding yourself together. As Christian leaders, we can project strength and spiritual insight while unknowingly carrying unmet wounds. But God, in His grace, never lets us carry those burdens alone—His Spirit is always working to bring us into truth and healing.

<u>When Healing Hurts First</u>

I had just returned from a deeply refreshing time in Canada—spiritually renewed, full of hope, and freshly aligned with God's direction for my life. I had connected with a spiritual father, Dr. Ralph, whose love and wisdom brought encouragement, correction, and perspective I didn't know I needed. After a week of prayer and fasting, I came back ready to share the joy with Jerome, one of my therapists—expecting a light, affirming conversation. Instead, what I received was a challenging session: I felt shot down, and holes were poked in all that joy. He began asking deep, searching questions—ones that unearthed things I hadn't considered. At first, I felt misunderstood and even a little frustrated, wondering why he couldn't just celebrate with me. Then I felt angry and wounded thinking he was suggesting I was trying to claim healing prematurely, as if I thought one spiritual high meant I was done with the process. I remember thinking, "What kind of counsellor is this? He doesn't understand me at all!" But I later realised Jerome wasn't dismissing my breakthrough at all. He was helping me uncover a deeper pattern - a major coping mechanism in my life. I have an instinct to keep pressing forward, which has helped me overcome a lot of real tough challenges in my life. But that same strength can also become a weakness if it causes me to bypass the deeper healing my heart truly needs. Jerome encouraged me to bring this to God directly—to ask Him where the roots of my struggles really came from. He shared his own story of how an unexpected event surfaced deeper fears from his history in war-torn countries and challenged me to invite the Holy Spirit to shine light on the hidden places of my own heart.

And I did. I set aside the frustration and simply prayed: "Lord, what's really going on in me?" The response was clear and surprising: "You're lonely." At first, I resisted—after all, I am blessed, I have a great family, friends and a good life. But as I prayed, the Holy Spirit began to connect the dots—showing how certain moments of disappointment, leadership pressure, grief, relationships and personal loss had quietly built patterns of emotional isolation. Without even realising it, parts of my heart had learned to function alone.

What I had once labelled as "just life", strength or independence was, in some cases, self-protection. I saw things in a different light. Patterns began to emerge, and I realised how this hidden ache had shaped my relationships and resilience over the years. This wasn't about solitude but surrender. In that moment of honesty and surrender, I could feel God peeling something away and something deep within me being healed and filled. Then came the words that marked me: "You are not alone." I had encountered Jesus before, but that night was different. I encountered Him on a whole other level. Though I lived alone, I was anything but alone. I was surrounded by God's tangible weighty presence, and just as powerfully, I sensed Him awakening something within me—a deep, sacred, unshakable knowing that I was seen, loved, and never alone.

More than a year later, that reality still anchors me. Turns out Jerome knew exactly what he was doing! That challenging session – the one I found most frustrating and almost dismissed - became the doorway to one of the most transformative encounters of my life. God used it to expose patterns that had quietly shaped my identity and leadership—and to replace them with a deep assurance of His presence. God has truly shown me that I'm not alone—and neither are you. If you walk with the Holy Spirit, He will lead you into the truth that heals, the wholeness that restores, and the transformation that lasts.

As Christian leaders, we can pick up wounds on the journey—or even before the journey begins. We may not notice them at first. We keep pressing forward, doing what's asked of us, pouring into others. But underneath the surface, those wounds can shape how we lead, relate, and even how we see ourselves and God. That's why we need the Holy Spirit—not just to empower our calling, but to transform our inner life.

Galatians 5:16 says "So I say, walk by the Spirit, and you will not gratify the desires of the flesh." In Scripture, the word "walk"—as in "walk by the Spirit"—comes from the Greek word 'peripateó'. It doesn't just mean to physically walk. It means to live, to conduct one's life, to frequent a place. Walking in the Bible always implied a pattern—a rhythm of life shaped by direction and identity. To walk by the Spirit means you live under His guidance, make decisions according to His voice, and operate by the supply of His power. This is not passive. It's intentional. It's daily. And it can only happen when we engage with the Holy Spirit.

This is where transformation truly begins. But I'm not sharing this just to inspire you —I'm sharing it to strengthen your walk. The Holy Spirit is willing to lead you—into healing, growth, and deep, lasting transformation. He's ready. But you must respond. You must participate. This isn't a passive process. Jesus said, "When the Spirit of truth comes, He will guide you into all truth" (John 16:13). That truth is not just theological—it's deeply personal. The Holy Spirit knows exactly what needs to be revealed, healed, restored, and transformed. He won't force you—but if you follow Him, He will lead you into the truth that sets you free. So, I want to give you three principles that will help you participate with the Holy Spirit—not just in emotional moments, but in the real, daily rhythm of your life. These truths are meant to be lived. And when they are, transformation becomes your reality.

Let's walk with Him.

1. Discomfort Leads to Discovery

Discomfort is often the birthplace of discovery. That's something my other therapist, Adrian, once told me—wisdom that has helped me learn to stay present in uncomfortable moments instead of rushing to escape them. He would often say, "You shall know the truth, and the truth may first make you feel miserable, but it sets you free." That perspective shifted how I see the wide range of emotions that rise when something deep inside me is stirred—sometimes without words to explain it. Can you relate? I've been there so many times—feeling something deeply but struggling to articulate it. If that's ever happened to you, you know it can be frustrating. But here's what I've learned: when we choose to walk through that inner discomfort—guided by God and surrounded by trusted voices—what we find on the other side can be genuinely life-changing. It takes courage, yes, but the fruit is transformation.

As you journey through the chapters of this book, I want you to consider how what you read will affect different parts of who you are. Each insight the Holy Spirit brings can impact at least one (and often more) of the following dimensions:

- Spiritual - Your connection with God
- Emotional - The way you feel and process emotions
- Psychological - Your mindset and thought patterns
- Physical - How your body responds to your inner and outer world
- Behavioural - The actions and habits you live out
- Relational - The way you connect with others

Let the discomfort speak. Let it lead you into what God is trying to reveal. That discovery could be the beginning of your growth, healing and transformation.

2. Don't Judge Your Emotions

You are not alone. This is the sacred truth the Holy Spirit brought me into—and it's the truth I want to speak over you.

As you go through the next chapters, I won't pretend it will be easy. They aren't meant to soothe your flesh or validate every feeling or default opinion you have. They are meant to sharpen, awaken, and call you deeper. You may face parts of yourself that are painful, confusing, ugly, or uncomfortable. You may feel angry, hurt, ashamed, or numb. But hear me: don't judge your emotions. Don't let them define you. Don't run from them. Instead, learn to sit with them—and sit with the Holy Spirit in them. Because if you do, He will guide you into all truth (John 8:32; John 16:13; 1 John 2:27). And that truth will set you free. The freedom might come with grieving first. Or wrestling. Or silence. Or conviction. And that's okay. The Holy Spirit is not afraid of your emotions. He wants to meet you in them and walk you through them.

3. Lean on The Holy Spirit: Bring Him Your Traumas, Triggers & Temptations

Whatever gets revealed in this journey—bring it to the Holy Spirit. Immediately. Don't wait. Don't overanalyse. Bring it as it comes. There is power in koinonia—true fellowship with God—and it is available to you in real time.

I'll be honest: I used to avoid certain kinds of discomfort. I would deal with challenges I was facing—up to a point—but when something felt overwhelming, I'd sometimes keep myself busy. I'd work, help others, watch movies, take on more projects… anything to distract myself from what was really going on inside. Sitting with pain or uncertainty wasn't my strength back then. But here's what I've learned: you can't truly walk in freedom if you cling to old coping mechanisms. Avoidance and distraction might numb the pain for a while, but it will never heal you. The Holy Spirit doesn't bypass your wounds—He enters them, and He does it with truth, love, and power.

One of the biggest shifts for me came when I stopped waiting for the "right time" to bring my pain to God. I began taking everything to Him in real time—frustrations, triggers, moments of temptation, times when I felt unsettled or vulnerable. I didn't just pray about the big events of my life; I invited Him into the small, hidden moments too – immediately. That kind of prayer wasn't passive—it was an active, daily dependence on His grace.

And something happened. The more I ran to Him in the moment, the more I found that His grace wasn't just helping me resist unhelpful patterns—it was healing deep places in my heart I didn't even know were still wounded. Prayer became a very deep well I could draw from at any time – finding myself in extended times of stillness, travail, prophetic intercession, and I discovered a new level of intimacy with the Holy Spirit. This may sound strange, but Jesus became my water (essential), and I felt like an astronaut exploring God in prayer. My prayer life deepened, my discernment sharpened, and I began to notice God speaking—not just in dramatic encounters—but even in my emotional responses. My capacity grew in every area: spiritually, emotionally, and mentally. It reminded me of

Matthew 7:5, where Jesus says that after you remove the log from your own eye, you will see clearly. That's exactly how it felt. The more I brought my weaknesses to Him, the clearer I could see—myself, others, nations, and God.

I can't stress enough: Pray about your pain. Bring your triggers to Him immediately. Don't wait for the right mood or moment. And trust this: He will comfort you. He will convict you. He will heal you. He will deliver you. And He will ignite what needs to be awakened inside of you. The Holy Spirit reveals not to shame—but to shape. Not to crush—but to restore. Not to reject—but to redeem. He is building you into the leader you were always meant to be.

<u>Living in the Spirit: Identity Over Emotion, Victory Over the Flesh</u>

The flesh is not merely our bodily impulses—it is the deep, internal desire to resist, leave or turn from the presence and word of God. Romans 8:7 teaches us that the mind governed by the flesh is hostile toward God and refuses to submit to Him. In contrast, the spirit is willing; it longs to remain in communion with the Father (Mathew 26:41). This battle between flesh and spirit is a reality for every believer. But here's the truth: you are <u>not</u> your flesh. Your identity is not rooted in your old nature but your position in Christ (Gal 2:20). The flesh may cry out, but the Spirit within you calls louder, and by that Spirit, you have the power to subject the desires of the flesh.

Victory over the flesh is not achieved through human willpower but through daily alignment with the Holy Spirit. Romans 8:5 shows that one of the key strategies is setting your mind on the things of the Spirit. What we focus on, we empower. Mindset determines direction. A renewed mind fuels a Spirit-led life. This isn't a passive activity—it requires intentionality. If your thoughts remain rooted in earthly desires, the flesh will thrive. But if your thoughts are anchored in spiritual truths, your inner life will reflect it.

Romans 8:13 reveals a vital truth about sanctification: it is a cooperative work between God and the believer. The verse says, "If by the Spirit you put to death the deeds of the body, you will live." Notice the language—'by the Spirit, you put to death'. This reveals divine partnership. God's role: Empowerment through the Holy Spirit. Your role: Actively confronting sin, habits, and wounds. God provides the power, but we must actively confront and dismantle sinful habits, patterns, and even unresolved wounds and emotional injuries. The Spirit empowers us, but we are still responsible for engaging the process of transformation.

Being "in the Spirit" is not an emotional mood—it's a settled identity. It is a permanent identity—a spiritual location—for those who belong to Christ. According to Romans 8:9, if the Spirit of God dwells in you, then you are no longer in the flesh, but in the Spirit. This means that your access to God's presence and power isn't determined by how you feel, but by who you are in Christ. Those who equate being in the Spirit with emotional intensity risk confusing mood with spiritual reality. They misinterpret their emotional state as their spiritual status. This is a dangerous misunderstanding because their spiritual position is held hostage to their fluctuating mood. You can be tired, discouraged, or even broken, yet still fully in the Spirit. Your spiritual life is not measured by emotional intensity, but by alignment and submission to God.

Finally, it's important to grasp that the indwelling power of sin is only overcome by the indwelling power of the Spirit. Romans 8:11 reminds us that the same Spirit who raised

Christ from the dead lives in us. This means we are never powerless. Through Him, our fleshly desires, sinful habits, and even deeply rooted emotional wounds can be healed and defeated. This is not a theory—it's a lived reality for those who walk in the Spirit.

Let's be people who understand that being "in the Spirit" is a permanent position of victory, not a fleeting moment of feeling. Let's daily set our minds on the Spirit, cooperate with the sanctifying work of God, and live in the fullness of our new identity. The battle may be real, but the Spirit within us is greater than the pull of the flesh.

Chapter 2 Reflections – You Are Not Alone: Held by the Holy Spirit

Memory Verse:

"And I will ask the Father, and he will give you another Helper, to be with you forever—even the Spirit of truth... You know him, for he dwells with you and will be in you." John 14:16–17

Personal Reflection Questions

1. "You Are Not Alone."

    - What does that truth stir in you right now? Do you believe it deeply—or do you simply know it intellectually?
    - What might be blocking you from experiencing the Holy Spirit as a present, active Helper?

2. The Power of Discomfort

    - Have you recently felt any emotional discomfort that you've avoided or dismissed?
    - What might the Holy Spirit be trying to show you through it?

3. Judging Emotions

    - Which emotions do you tend to judge or suppress (e.g., anger, sadness, shame)?
    - How could sitting with those emotions alongside the Holy Spirit open up space for deeper healing?

4. Avoidance & Coping Mechanisms

- What are your "go-to" avoidance tactics when things feel overwhelming (e.g., scrolling, overworking, staying busy)?
- How do those habits affect your connection with God and others?

5. Immediate Surrender

- Reflect on the statement: "Bring it to the Holy Spirit immediately."
- What would change in your life if you practised immediate surrender in moments of pain, temptation, or confusion?

6. Grace in the Midst of Temptation

- Are there areas of temptation or emotional struggle where you've been trying to manage things in your own strength?
- How might proactive, Spirit-led prayer open you to receive more grace?

7. Prophetic Discernment through Emotion

- Have you ever experienced God speaking to you through your emotions? What happened?
- What would it look like to treat your emotional life as a space for spiritual revelation, not just reaction?

8. Transformation through Partnership

- What specific area of your life do you feel the Holy Spirit is inviting you to walk more closely with Him in?
- What might participation look like—practically—in that area this week?

Closing Prayer

Holy Spirit, I invite You into every part of me—especially the places I avoid. Teach me to bring things to You immediately. I don't want to numb or distract myself from what You are trying to reveal. Give me the courage to sit with You in discomfort, and the grace to pray without ceasing. Heal what needs healing. Awaken what needs awakening. And shape me into the person You've called me to be. I trust You, and I choose to walk with You. In Jesus' name, Amen.

Chapter 3

Developmental Foundations of Pastoral Vulnerability

A leader's early formation profoundly shapes their ministry. Acknowledging vulnerability is not weakness, it is a doorway to authentic growth and godly leadership. Almost every leader's story begins in the same place: family. This is the heart of this chapter. Whether we're conscious of it or not, our early family systems play a central role in shaping our development. I remember my therapist Adrian once challenged my presentation of my "perfect childhood''. Not that I actual believed it was perfect – I enjoyed my childhood - but I felt uncomfortable because I didn't want the acknowledgement of imperfection to present as a lack of gratitude or dishonour of my family. I have been privileged to have such a loving and supportive mother and a good relationship with my brothers and sister since childhood. Yet I learned that I had downplayed the emotional impact of certain early experiences—times when I felt unsafe around certain people or longed for a deeper sense of connection with my father (may he rest in peace). Adrian's aim wasn't to dishonour my family (they're genuinely great people), but to help me understand that even in loving environments, gaps can exist that influence how we show up later in life. These gaps can unintentionally contribute to patterns in adulthood. All families do beautiful, meaningful things. But all families also fall short in certain ways. Both realities shape us. What we don't acknowledge from our formation can often show up in our future, especially in leadership.

For many, the idea of a vulnerable leader-especially a pastor-feels like a contradiction. But a contradiction simply means two seemingly inconsistent things coexisting. Pastors are anointed, gifted, and called. And pastors are also human-vulnerable, growing, and unfinished. That's not an indictment; it's reality. Yet, this truth is often ignored, spiritualised, or outright denied in ministry culture. Why? Because many leaders have never examined how the dynamics of their family of origin shaped their identity, emotional habits, or relational patterns. Like anyone else, pastors can carry childhood wounds and coping strategies into adulthood-and into their ministries. Add those early vulnerabilities to the pressures of ministry, and the weight can become unbearable. The anointing doesn't erase humanity. Gifting doesn't cancel growth. Position doesn't eliminate pain.

Family: God's First Classroom

God designed the family to be the primary environment where identity is formed, and values are passed on (Genesis 18:19; Genesis 27; Hebrews 11:20). It's through our families that we're meant to receive blessing, stability, and training for life. But when the family structure is broken or imbalanced, our development often follows suit. Earle Jr. & Laaser (2002) outline several key aspects of family systems that significantly impact personal and leadership formation:

1. Boundaries

Healthy families establish clear, safe boundaries. Too rigid, and they prevent connection. Too loose, and they invite chaos. Both extremes create dysfunction that can later affect leadership decisions and relational health.

2. Communication

Some families model healthy emotional expression, while others suppress it entirely. In some Christian households, expressing emotions like grief, anger, or sadness may be labelled as weakness or "a lack of faith." Over time, this creates emotional illiteracy that follows us into ministry.

3. Responsibility & Accountability

Families teach us how to own our mistakes-or avoid them. Phrases like "You were right," or "I'm sorry" model humility and promote reconciliation. Leaders who were never taught this can struggle to admit fault, accept correction, or build healthy teams.

4. Roles

We all take on roles in our families: the peacemaker, the performer, the problem-solver. These roles may help us survive in childhood but become liabilities when unconsciously carried into ministry. Without reflection, pastors may repeat those roles in how they relate to their churches, employers with their employees or parents with their children etc.

5. Coping Strategies

Every family experiences stress. How we learn to cope-whether through humour, overachievement, avoidance, or addiction-shapes us deeply. Those strategies can evolve into ministry masks: hyper-productivity, people-pleasing, or emotional detachment.

Core Beliefs & Hidden Scripts

Beneath our behaviours lie core beliefs-assumptions we hold about ourselves, others, and God. These beliefs can be healthy or harmful, rooted in truth or trauma. Psychologically, these are known as presuppositions-mental rules we follow without even realising it.

Here are some examples of common negative beliefs leaders carry:

- "I'm alone. People can't be trusted."

Often formed in unpredictable or inconsistent homes, this belief creates guarded independence and emotional isolation in leadership.

- "I must be perfect, or I'll be rejected."

Perfectionism is one of the greatest weights pastors carry. This pressure often originates in childhood experiences of conditional acceptance-and is amplified by ministry expectations.

- "If I speak my needs, I'll lose love."

Leaders who avoid vulnerability or hard conversations may carry the unspoken rule that expressing their true thoughts and feelings leads to rejection. These scripts must be brought to light not to condemn, but to heal and be reshaped.

The Benefits of Facing Your Past

God offers an amazing (and yet, painful) invitation: to face your story. The parts that are dark, confusing, or shameful are often the very places God wants to redeem. If we are willing to confront these vulnerable spaces, He promises to walk with us, heal us, and even use our stories to set others free.

1. Breaking the Power of the Past

Whether we are aware or not – whatever is suppressed within us unconsciously will be expressed in our behaviour. When we are aware of the root and expression of our trauma, phobias, limiting beliefs or dysfunctional behaviour, the hidden demonic power begins to diminish. You will be surprised that God can use your greatest weakness to be a source where God's power flows through you! Paul's story is an inspiration to me (read 2 Corinthians 12:8-12). His struggle was not a source of shame but a source of humility and godly boasting because God's grace operated powerfully through his weaknesses. Once I recognised some of my own trauma-based tendencies – people please tendencies, 'massaging the truth' (withholding information out of fear of rejection), negative self-criticism- I became more empowered not to feed these behaviours and be proactive about overcoming them! I learned to humbly seek Gods help each day, which helped me overcome challenges from my past.

2. Your History Becomes His Story

This is a play on words, but it simply means God can use your story in His service to others. God never wastes pain and neither should we. The very things that once made you hide in shame can become a testimony and instrument He uses to set others free (Revelation 12:10). I used to feel embarrassed by the "messy" parts of my story—until God reminded me that Jesus was born in a manger. A messy place. That wasn't by accident; it was a divine statement. The doctrine of the Incarnation is prophetic, profound, practical, and missional. Why would God choose to show up in such a messy and ordinary space? To teach us that

God can show up anywhere. Jesus came into the world through a place no one expected, reminding us that we can't underestimate what God can birth through the messy places of our lives. What if your deepest and darkest pain is exactly where God wants to shine His light the brightest? Your story will either be used against you by the enemy—or it will become a powerful weapon in the hands of God to defeat the enemy.

Five Steps to Confront Your Early Formation

This work isn't easy. It will require courage, patience, prayer, support and sometimes professional help. But if you commit to it, you'll begin a journey of deep transformation that affects not just you, but everyone you lead.

Here are five practical steps:

1. Organise your thoughts by naming your emotions.

Journaling, counselling, or spiritual mentors can help with this.

2. Use a genogram to explore your family history.

A genogram is a visual map of your family tree across generations. It's a powerful tool for identifying repeated behaviours, patterns, traumas, and themes. See Appendix 1 at the back of the book for an example and questionnaire to guide you.

3. Seek guidance from trustworthy mentors or professionals.

Don't do this alone. A therapist, spiritual mentor, or emotionally healthy and mature peer can help you navigate this process with grace and truth.

4. <u>Prayerfully identify negative scripts.</u>

Ask God to show you the hidden beliefs that are shaping your decisions and relationships.

5. <u>Pursue deliverance.</u>

For some, healing will involve spiritual deliverance-breaking agreements with fear, shame, rejection, or pride etc. The Holy Spirit is fully committed to your freedom.

Take Your Loved Ones with You

At some point I'd sat down with my mother and, in one of the most honest and humbling conversations we've had, she shared openly about both the strengths and the struggles that run through our family line. We prayed together, naming generational patterns and breaking cycles that had affected us all—some knowingly, some unknowingly. My mother has always been one of my closest relationships. She's been my number one supporter—praying for me consistently, offering wise counsel, attending the church I pastored and cheering me on through every high and low. Because of her insight and steady support, I've been able to build a successful life—becoming a property investor and running a supported living company. I genuinely believe I wouldn't be the man I am today without her. And yet, through this process of reflection and prayer, I was hit with a painful realisation: although she had always been present and available, I hadn't always invited her into my deeper struggles. I didn't always make full use of her support or carry her with me on the journey in the ways I truly could have. That realisation hurt her—and it hurt me too. It's a strange and sobering truth in ministry: sometimes we pour ourselves out for people who may walk away the moment things get hard. And in doing so, we can unconsciously neglect or deprioritise those who have been there for us unconditionally. Not because we don't love them—but because the pace and pressure of ministry can blur our vision and distort our priorities. That conversation with my mother changed both of us. It took our relationship to another level. I began to see my family history through clearer eyes and deeper prophetic revelation—identifying patterns, tracing the roots of certain core beliefs, and recognising the childhood roles I had carried into adulthood and even ministry. I often tell my mother this: If I could do this life again, I would choose you again. And I mean every word. When I shared this journey with my brothers, they weren't surprised. They could relate. They too were pursuing personal growth and healing. This process of transformation was no longer a solo mission—it became a family journey. So, to every pastor, leader, and person called by God: don't let the demands of ministry cause you to miss those who love you the most. Life gets busy. Ministry can be disorienting. But I want to encourage you—take your loved ones with you as much as possible. For those whose biological family are not safe but hostile. I see you. God sees you. Whoever you call your loved ones - let them in. Let them walk with you. Healing is not just for you; it can be for your whole family. Let your transformation ripple outward—and watch how God not only heals you, but the generations around you.

Final Thought: You're a Person Before You're a Leader

Stop saying, "I'm a pastor—I shouldn't feel this way," or "I don't have the right to struggle." Before God ever gave you a platform, He gave you a soul. You are a person first—not a function. You're not just a leader; you're a human being made in God's image. When you stop judging your emotions and start paying attention to them, you open yourself up to the refining, healing work of the Holy Spirit—to clarify what's confusing, contextualise what's painful, heal what's broken, and reveal what's hidden. This is more than self-care. This is war. There is a battle for your soul, your identity, and your legacy. The enemy would love for your vulnerabilities to remain hidden, so they can eventually become the place of your downfall. But when you walk in truth—with God, yourself, and others—you protect those tender places instead of allowing them to become targets. And here's the beautiful part: what you confront today doesn't just change your future—it can change your family's future. We may have learned some of these lessons later, but we can teach the next generation earlier. We can model emotional honesty, spiritual depth, and healthy leadership so our children and spiritual sons and daughters can walk in greater freedom. So, take a step. Don't just think about this—act on it. Get a notebook. Start prayerfully mapping out your genogram—your family tree. Ask the Holy Spirit to help you identify the patterns, roles, and unspoken scripts that have shaped you. Write them down. Bring them into your prayers, your journal, your conversations, and your discipleship journey. Let this be the beginning—not just of deeper ministry, but of deep personal wholeness. Because when you are transformed, your leadership is too—and so is your legacy.

Chapter 3 Reflections - Developmental Foundations of Pastoral Vulnerability

Memory Verse:

"Search me, O God, and know my heart! Try me and know my thoughts! And see if there be any grievous way in me and lead me in the way everlasting." — Psalm 139:23–24

Personal Reflection Questions

1. Formed by Family

- What unspoken beliefs or roles did you take on as a child that might still be influencing how you lead today?
- When you reflect on your upbringing, what strengths do you carry into leadership? What struggles?
- Are there areas of your family history you've idealised or overlooked that may need honest exploration?

2. Unlearning the "Perfect Leader" Myth

- Do you believe vulnerability is a threat to your credibility—or an invitation to deeper authenticity?
- How comfortable are you with admitting your weaknesses or emotional needs to others? To yourself? To God?

3. Core Beliefs and Hidden Scripts

- What internal scripts or negative beliefs have you noticed repeating in your leadership or relationships (e.g., "I must be perfect," "People will leave," "I'm on my own")?
- Where might those beliefs have come from? What would it look like to bring them before the Holy Spirit for truth and healing?

4. Take Your Loved Ones with You

- Who has supported you most consistently in life or ministry? Have you intentionally included them in your journey of growth and healing?
- Have the pressures of ministry ever caused you to neglect the people who love you unconditionally?
- What practical steps can you take to invite your spouse, children, parents, or siblings to walk with you in this season of transformation?

5. Turning History into His Story

- Are there parts of your story you still feel ashamed to share? How might God want to use them as a testimony?
- In what ways could your personal healing unlock freedom for others in your family or ministry?

6. From Reflection to Action

- Have you ever used a genogram to prayerfully examine your family story? What patterns or spiritual dynamics might the Holy Spirit be highlighting?
- What would it look like to start this process practically—today? Have you taken the step of writing down your emotional triggers, family patterns, and spiritual battles?

Closing Prayer

Holy Spirit, I invite You into the places that shaped me—both beautiful and broken. Help me to stop running from what You want to heal. Show me the unspoken scripts, roles, and beliefs that are still guiding my heart and my leadership. I surrender them to You. I ask for the courage to reflect honestly, the humility to seek help, and the faith to believe You can redeem my history for Your glory. Let my transformation be a legacy. Heal me not just for me—but for the generations after me. In Jesus' name, Amen.

Chapter 4

When Leaders Drift: The High Cost of Misalignment

When leaders become misaligned with God, within themselves, and with their God-given mission, it always comes at a cost—a deep spiritual, emotional, and relational cost. This misalignment doesn't just affect the leader personally; it ripples outward, impacting families, teams, churches, and ultimately, the integrity of God's mission on the earth.

To be misaligned is to be "out of correct position or improperly adjusted." When this happens in a leader's life, it often starts subtly—through spiritual drift, unresolved emotional pain, or blurred purpose. Over time, the consequences compound: burnout replaces passion, activity replaces productivity, confusion clouds conviction, and relationships become strained or dysfunctional. What once was proactive Spirit-led influence turns into reactive leadership—often masked by activity but lacking intimacy with God. Before we can truly understand the power and freedom that come from divine alignment, we must first confront the real consequences of its absence. The story of David and Bathsheba is not just one of moral failure; it is a sobering portrait of what happens when a leader loses alignment with God, with himself, and with his purpose.

This chapter is not written to condemn, but to awaken. Every pastor and leader must understand that misalignment costs more than we can see at first glance. It affects our decisions, relationships, integrity, productivity and ability to discern God's voice. And perhaps most tragically, it hinders the very people and mission we've been entrusted to lead and protect. Even if you're not in full-time ministry, these principles still apply. Whether you're a parent, business owner, student, or volunteer—anyone entrusted with influence must guard their alignment with God, because misalignment will always impact those around you and the purpose you were created to fulfil. Let's take a closer look at David's story—not to judge him, but to learn from him. May we recognise the warning signs in our own lives and return to the place of alignment before the cost becomes too high.

5 Consequences of Misalignment

1.Misalignment Distorts Discernment: Misjudging Seasons

Scripture Reference: 2 Samuel 11:1 "*In the spring of the year, the time when kings go out to battle... But David remained at Jerusalem.*"

One of the most dangerous consequences of spiritual misalignment is a distortion of discernment—the ability to sense, understand and participate in what God is doing in a particular time or season. Discernment enables leaders to know when to fight, when to rest, when to speak, and when to be silent. But when a leader drifts from alignment with God, that clarity becomes clouded. David's decision to remain in Jerusalem during a time of war reveals more than a leadership oversight; it shows a distortion of discernment. The text emphasises that this was the season when kings were expected to go out to battle—yet David, a battle-tested warrior and king, chose to stay behind. While his recent military success (2 Samuel 10:14) may have offered a reason for strategic rest, the timing was off. David misread the season, and that misreading was a sign of deeper misalignment.

Misalignment skews perspective. David's first mistake wasn't adultery-it was absence. What feels like a well-earned rest can be a retreat from responsibility. Discernment, when filtered through unresolved exhaustion, trauma, or pride, becomes compromised. Leaders begin to interpret seasons based on their feelings rather than God's direction. Many leaders today face similar moments. Leadership pressures, unprocessed emotions, or spiritual fatigue can cause them to discern through the lens of self, not the Spirit. You may still be active in ministry, still making decisions—but your sense of timing, placement, and purpose is off. That's the cost of misalignment.

Personal Reflection: Is your discernment being guided by divine wisdom or emotional fatigue? Are you misjudging your season because you're out of spiritual or emotional rhythm?

True discernment comes from abiding in God. Without it, even the most experienced leaders will find themselves in the wrong place at the wrong time—just like David. Misalignment doesn't always announce itself with loud rebellion; sometimes, it shows up quietly in subtle delays, misplaced rest, or poor timing. And when discernment is distorted, danger is not far behind.

<u>Strong, Sacrificial… and Struggling</u>

For me, it was the opposite of David's situation. David was meant to be at war, but he stayed behind to rest. In my case, I should have stopped to rest, but I kept pushing forward. Earlier in the preface, I shared about a significant relationship that ended a few years ago—a season that left me deeply injured. Have you ever been so wounded by someone's decision that it didn't just cause pain in the moment, but also brushed up against older, unhealed places in your heart? That was me. This is not about blaming the other person; relationships are complex, and it takes two. But I am speaking honestly about the impact it had on me.

I felt the pressure to keep going. In ministry, the demands don't pause for your pain. They come in waves—marriage crises, counselling sessions, hospital visits, emergencies, mediation meetings, sermon preparation—all while managing a business and a staff team. I told my close circle, including Dr. Sharon, about what had happened, and I fully intended to take a couple of weeks off. But the concept of an extended rest or sabbatical didn't fit my inner framework at the time. I would take the occasional Monday off, but even that wasn't always consistent. Somewhere deep inside, my core beliefs about strength, sacrifice, and resilience wouldn't let me fully slow down.

The truth is, I was hurt - badly. I knew I was carrying a deep wound. But I defaulted to what I knew: minimise it, push through, and serve. It sounds noble, but it's risky. When we don't give ourselves permission to heal, we become vulnerable—not just emotionally, but spiritually and mentally. And like David, I wasn't where I should have been—but for me, it was rest I resisted, not war.

2. Misalignment Breeds Dysfunction: Impure Motives & Toxic Relationships

Dysfunctional relationships are often the fruit of a misaligned heart in leadership. In 2 Samuel 11:2, we read, "*It happened, late one afternoon, when David arose from his couch... he saw from the roof a woman bathing; and the woman was very beautiful.*" With his army away at war, David-out of alignment and isolated-found himself vulnerable to temptation. Bathsheba was likely completing a purification ritual after her menstrual cycle (Leviticus

15:19-24), making it clear that when she later conceives (2 Samuel 11:5), the child could not be her husband Uriah's.

David's decision to summon her wasn't about care or concern, it was desire, cloaked in kingly privilege. The authority of his position couldn't justify the adultery that followed. This moment reveals what happens when emotional needs and desires are left unsubmitted to God. Philippians 4:19 tells us that God supplies all our needs, but if we don't trust Him with our emotional hunger, our unmet desires can twist our motives – even in ministry.

Unchecked emotions don't just disappear; they distort. We may still be preaching, leading, or counselling, singing, evangelising but beneath the surface, those unaddressed desires are influencing our interactions-sometimes in subtle ways, sometimes in obvious toxic ones. Even good actions can be fuelled by wrong motives. A desire for validation might drive someone to build a bigger ministry or scale a business—not because God led them, but because their worth is tied to outcomes and applause. A leader might launch a new program, take on speaking engagements, or pursue high-profile partnerships not from divine direction, but from a need to be seen, needed, or admired. In business, a person may hire certain people or chase strategic deals out of insecurity or ego rather than wisdom. The fruit may look successful for a while, but if the root is misaligned, eventually the dysfunction will show—through burnout, relational tension, or spiritual compromise.

That's why unsubmitted desires are dangerous: they can camouflage themselves in productivity or spiritual language while quietly driving decisions that detour us from God's best.

Take Mark, for example. He led an evangelistic ministry but had a deep, unsubmitted lust toward women he was attracted to. Over time, his team noticed a pattern: he would focus more evangelistic energy on women who fit his preference on the street. When they gently raised their concerns, Mark grew defensive and denied any issue. His unsubmitted desire had begun shaping his ministry interactions, breeding dysfunction.

There's a difference between suppression and submission.

- Submission means surrendering your will and emotions to God, trusting Him to meet your needs with grace and wisdom.

- Suppression means stuffing those needs down, hoping they'll stay quiet. But whatever you suppress, you'll eventually express-often in ways that bring harm to you and others. That's exactly what happened with David-and I can relate.

When Pain Doesn't Pause

A few months after the breakup, I was still trying to adjust my mind and emotions to that change when I got a call from my friend's wife one evening—he was going in for surgery. We ended up staying at the hospital for seven days. His wife and close family literally slept there, while the rest of us went home at night and returned each day. When he passed away, it felt like a hammer hit my soul. The next day, I had to tell my team and church. We still had a prayer meeting scheduled, and friends came to stand with us—but my heart was heavy. Make no mistake—others had even more reason than I did to grieve. But I'm sharing this because it highlights something so many leaders experience: life doesn't pause for your pain. Ministry keeps going. People still need answers. The business still needs management. Sunday still comes. And because of that, we can easily fall into the illusion that we'll address our internal wounds "when things calm down"—a time that rarely comes. During that season, I was supporting my team, serving the congregation, preaching weekly, and managing business responsibilities—it didn't stop. And I want to be clear: there is never an excuse for sin. In fact, the Holy Spirit taught me years later that when there is an excuse for sin there is an open door. Yet I'm saying this because I want to be real with you about what I was thinking and feeling back then. I was deeply depleted. I told myself, "If I stop now, I will fall apart. The church needs me. The business depends on me." On the surface, it sounded noble. But in reality, I was silencing what my soul was screaming and listening to distorted core beliefs instead. So much was happening at once—it was unreal. I slipped into "just survive" mode. Have you ever been there? Where you can still feel, but at the same time, parts of you feel numb? Partly because too much is happening to process at the same time. I refused to abandon those around me—I wanted to sacrifice myself for them. On the surface, it was noble. But underneath, I abandoned myself and the internal misalignment was quietly creating more problems, ones that would only become visible over time. Sometimes the most dangerous sacrifices are the ones that look spiritual but are rooted in unhealed wounds. In my case, what looked like dedication was actually being fuelled by a mixture of genuine love, exhaustion, unresolved grief, and neglected needs. Over time, that internal misalignment began shaping how I related and made decisions. It's a sobering reminder: if we don't address what's beneath the surface, it will eventually affect what's above it.

3. Misalignment Compromises Integrity: Fighting the Light

When leaders fall into misalignment, they often find themselves doing the unthinkable: fighting against their own integrity to keep their sin hidden or managed. This is the tragedy we see unfold in 2 Samuel 11:6-13. David, a man after God's own heart, begins orchestrating a cover-up, and the target becomes one of his own loyal warriors-Uriah the Hittite. Uriah wasn't just any soldier; he was one of David's mighty men (2 Samuel 23:39), a general known for his bravery, loyalty, and moral discipline. Even his name is prophetic-"Uriah" means "Yahweh is my light." And light, in Scripture, often represents truth, purity, and God's presence. Uriah stood for everything David was drifting from. According to the customs and laws of the time (see 1 Samuel 21:5, Exodus 19:15, Leviticus 15:18), soldiers abstained from sexual intimacy during active duty, considering it a form of ritual consecration. So, when David summoned Uriah home in hopes of using him to mask Bathsheba's pregnancy, Uriah refused to compromise. He remained aligned in conviction and duty, even when David tried to manipulate him.

Uriah becomes a model for three things: integrity, consecration, and illumination.

- Integrity is the internal strength to remain whole and undivided under pressure.
- Consecration is choosing holiness in public and private.
- Illumination is walking in God's light, refusing to be shaped by darkness.

David, on the other hand, was now actively working against all three. Instead of repenting, he tried to bend Uriah's principles to cover his own sin. But when Uriah wouldn't bend, David broke further. This is the danger of unchecked misalignment: when we no longer fight the flesh-we start fighting the light. We resist conviction. We suppress truth. We attack the very people or standards that once inspired us. I've known what it means at times to fight against my Uriah, my conscience. It sounds shocking, but it's subtle. It happens when you justify a compromised boundary. When you silence that nagging conviction. When you withdraw from the people who represent accountability. Leaders, beware. Uriah remained on duty-even in Jerusalem, even when no one else would know. May God make us leaders who stay on duty wherever they are, in the pulpit or marketplace, in public or in private. And may we be humble enough to recognise when we're no longer resisting sin but resisting the light.

4. Misalignment Multiplies Sin: From Cover-Up to Conspiracy

When a leader continues to ignore the signs of internal misalignment, sin doesn't stay contained, it multiplies. The next step after cover-up is often conspiracy. We see this unfold in 2 Samuel 11:14-25. After David's attempts to manipulate Uriah fail, he faces a decision: will he come clean, or will he escalate his deception? Tragically, David chooses the latter. Instead of killing the sin at its root, he kills the man who represents his integrity. Uriah-the symbol of faithfulness, loyalty, and truth-becomes a casualty of David's unchecked desires. What began as lust spiralled into manipulation. What couldn't be hidden became a crime. David now uses his God-given authority to orchestrate a murder. That's the power of misalignment-unchecked; it makes leaders capable of justifying the most destructive choices under the illusion of control. A conspiracy, by definition, is "a secret plan by a group to do something unlawful or harmful." That's exactly what happens: David involves Joab, one of his generals, turning what should have been a trusted relationship into a covert alliance in sin. Joab follows orders, but the cost is irreversible. A good man dies, a woman grieves, and a child is born into the mess. Misalignment doesn't just affect the leader-it infects every environment they influence.

This is what can happen when desires go unsubmitted, when pride remains uncrucified:

- We justify harmful decisions.
- We misuse our influence to manage or control outcomes.
- We shift from servants to self-preservers.

I can relate to David to a certain extent—let me be clear, I haven't killed anyone! But I can admit there have been moments in leadership where I could have navigated situations with greater wisdom and transparency. Sometimes my aim was to protect someone's privacy; other times, if I'm being honest, I wanted to protect my own reputation. While the motives were noble, I learned that without full submission to God, even good intentions can create unnecessary confusion, hurt and strain trust. Those quiet decisions—made behind the scenes—taught me that when we prioritise perception over authenticity, we risk crossing lines that compromise the very trust leadership is built on. Trust is more than a currency—it's a calling. Romans 6:13 reminds us: "Do not offer any part of yourself to sin as an instrument of wickedness but rather offer yourselves to God… as instruments of righteousness." We aren't called to perfection, but we are called to submission. Leadership influence was never meant for image management—it's entrusted to us for the consecration and transformation of those we serve.

5. Misalignment Destroys Perspective: Losing Sight of Eternity

One of the most dangerous consequences of misalignment is the loss of an eternal perspective.

"*When the wife of Uriah heard that Uriah her husband was dead, she lamented over her husband. And when the mourning was over, David sent and brought her to his house, and she became his wife and bore him a son. But the thing that David had done displeased the Lord.*"—2 Samuel 11:26–27

David had managed to cover the situation in the eyes of people—he looked like a compassionate king who took a grieving widow into his home. But from heaven's view, he was far from righteous. "But the thing that David had done displeased the Lord." That single line pierces the illusion. What looked like compassion was actually rebellion. This is the power of perspective—human approval can never substitute for divine accountability. To live with an eternal perspective means we align our choices with God's timeless truth. Ecclesiastes 3:11 says God has "set eternity in the human heart." That means our lives and decisions carry eternal weight—even when they feel temporary. But when leaders become misaligned with God, their perspective shifts. Like David, they become more focused on short-term damage control than long-term spiritual integrity. They begin to sacrifice the ultimate for the immediate—temporary relief at the expense of lasting righteousness.

I won't pretend I've never faced the temptation to protect my own image. There have been moments in leadership where I leaned toward managing perception instead of fully surrendering the outcome to God. Have you ever caught yourself softening the truth—not out of some malicious intention, but to make it more acceptable to yourself or others? If so, you're not alone. (And if you've never felt that… it may be worth asking if pride is keeping you from seeing it!).

The writer of Hebrews warns us about the subtle deceptive nature of sin (Hebrews 3:13)—how it works quietly, numbing the heart, dulling our fear of God, and shifting our focus from Christ and eternity to comfort and control. Sometimes, what feels like noble sacrifice—pushing through pain, postponing personal healing, or prioritising others to our own detriment—can actually be disobedience to God and resistance to what the Holy Spirit is asking us to face. We might call it selflessness, but Heaven may call it misalignment. The Spirit knows the true cost of misalignment—how it distorts judgement, opens doors to compromise, and damages not only us, but those entrusted to us. What we delay in dealing with emotionally or spiritually, He's already urging us to confront. Not out of shame—but because He sees what's coming down the road if we don't. David's downward spiral didn't begin with murder—it began with misalignment. And by the end of this chapter, what stands out most isn't his status, but the absence of the fear of the Lord. As leaders, this isn't just about our personal walk. When we lose perspective, it impacts our families, our communities, and those God has entrusted to us. The decisions we make today will echo in eternity. That reality should keep us both humble and aligned.

Realignment Begins with Repentance: Returning to God

In attempting to cover his sin, David only compounded it. By the time the dust settled, he had broken multiple commandments — the 10th (coveting, Exodus 20:17), the

7th (adultery, Exodus 20:14), and the 6th (murder, Exodus 20:13). Though David may have felt he'd successfully avoided exposure, the Lord had been silently watching the entire time. God's silence was not absence — it was mercy. The same God who had shepherded David from the fields of Bethlehem to the throne of Israel was still at work, patiently giving space for repentance. But when David remained unresponsive, God, in His grace, intervened through the prophet Nathan (2 Samuel 12:1-14).

Nathan's approach was filled with wisdom — he didn't confront David directly at first. Instead, he presented a fictional legal case, inviting David to render judgement. Unknowingly, David condemned himself. It was only then that his eyes opened, and he confessed, "I have sinned against the Lord!" (2 Samuel 12:13). It was a moment of genuine repentance. Still, the consequences of his choices could not be erased. To realign with God, David had to start with true repentance. That meant taking full ownership of his sin. No blame shifting. No spiritual excuses. Just broken honesty before a holy God. Jesus began His earthly ministry with the words, "Repent and believe the good news" (Mark 1:15). This reminds us that true belief is born out of repentance — not just sorrow over the results of sin, but a surrender of the rebellion itself. Real repentance is not about escaping consequences but about returning to the One we've drifted from. It is about dethroning self and re-enthroning Christ. David's repentance brought about realignment — but not without cost. In Psalm 51:14–17, we get a vulnerable glimpse into David's inner torment. "Deliver me from the guilt of bloodshed…" he cries. Have you ever struggled to forgive yourself? David did. He was haunted by the reality that his misalignment had cost someone else their life. That's the sobering truth — our spiritual misalignment, if left unchecked, affects more than just us. It can wound, confuse, and even destroy others. But here is the good news: God is merciful. He doesn't just forgive sin — He delivers us from the guilt, shame, and condemnation that try to linger after repentance. You don't have to live with the emotional residue of failure. You can be free. Don't just repent — receive forgiveness. Let God realign your heart, renew your spirit, and restore your leadership from the inside out.

Conclusion: If Drift Has a Cost, Alignment Has a Reward

Leaders, let David's story sober us and sanctify us. Misalignment is dangerous—and no one is above it. Be honest about your needs. Don't cover what God wants to cleanse. Your alignment with God is not just for you—it affects everyone you lead. This passage doesn't just serve as a historical lesson; it gives us a practical theology of sin as it relates to leadership. While there are many warning signs of misalignment, these are the ones the Holy Spirit impressed on my heart to emphasise. This is not to condemn—but to awaken. Alignment is not a one-time achievement—it's a daily decision. And when necessary, we must be humble and wise enough to step away temporarily to address what's happening within. Better to pause and heal than to push forward and harm. If the cost of misalignment is this high and far-reaching, then consider the power and fruit of true alignment—clarity, health, authority, wholeness and peace. Not just for you, but for the people, teams, family, business, and ministries God has entrusted to you.

Chapter 4 Reflections - When Leaders Drift: The High Cost of Misalignment

Memory Verse:

"Whoever conceals their sins does not prosper, but the one who confesses and renounces them finds mercy.' — Proverbs 28:13

Personal Reflection Questions

1. Misalignment Distorts Discernment: Misjudging Seasons

    - Am I discerning this current season through God's wisdom or through my emotional exhaustion, grief, or pride?
    - Have I stayed in places I was supposed to leave—or kept moving when I was supposed to rest?
    - Who or what has been influencing my sense of timing lately—God, pressure, pain, or fear?

2. Misalignment Breeds Dysfunction: Impure Motives & Toxic Relationships

    - Are there emotional or relational needs in my life that I've suppressed instead of surrendered to God?
    - Where might unmet desires be subtly influencing my leadership decisions or relational boundaries?

- What patterns (emotional, relational, or behavioural) have I started to justify, even if I know they're unhealthy?

3. <u>Misalignment Compromises Integrity: Fighting the Light</u>

   - Have I started hiding, spinning, or covering parts of my life that once were open to God and others?
   - Is there a "Uriah" in my life—someone whose integrity or truth I've been avoiding, resenting, or resisting?
   - Am I still resisting sin—or have I begun resisting light, truth, and accountability?

4. <u>Misalignment Multiplies Sin: From Cover-Up to Conspiracy</u>

   - Have I ever ignored the warning signs of misalignment in my life or leadership?
   - In what areas have I allowed manipulation or secrecy to take root instead of seeking God's light?
   - Am I using my influence to serve others—or to protect an image?
   - Have I ever involved others in a decision or plan that compromised their integrity or mine?
   - How have I justified actions that, deep down, I knew were not right?
   - What are the costs—relational, spiritual, emotional—of my unaddressed misalignment?

5. <u>Misalignment Destroys Perspective: Losing Sight of Eternity</u>

- When have I prioritised short-term relief over long-term spiritual integrity?
- How do I respond when I feel the pressure to manage optics rather than walk in truth?
- Have I ever tried to "make it right" outwardly without first repenting inwardly?
- How do I discern the difference between noble sacrifice and subtle disobedience?
- Is my leadership grounded in an eternal perspective—or shaped by temporary fears and expectations?
- What have I convinced myself "wasn't that serious," that actually needs confronting with honesty?
- In what ways might I be numb to the Spirit's promptings?

6. <u>Realignment Begins with Repentance: Returning to God</u>

- Am I more concerned with avoiding consequences than being truly right with God?
- Have I taken full ownership of my choices without blaming others or offering spiritual-sounding excuses?
- How do I respond when someone (like Nathan) lovingly confronts me with truth?

- Do I believe I am truly forgiven—or am I still carrying the guilt of past failures?
- How might God be calling me to dethrone self and re-enthrone Christ in a specific area of my life?

7. General Leadership Reflection

- Am I leading with integrity or managing impressions?
- Do I truly trust God with the consequences of full transparency?
- How does my leadership reflect the fear of the Lord?
- What does repentance look like practically for me today—not just emotionally, but in action?

Closing Prayer

Father, I come before You with a heart laid bare. I confess—I've allowed misalignment to take hold. I've let compromise multiply where conviction should've taken root. I've covered what I should've confessed, manipulated when I should've submitted. I've misused what You gave me, placing image over integrity. I've lived for the immediate, forgetting the eternal. And I've hardened my heart when You were gently calling me back. Father, I'm done avoiding. I don't want to manage appearances—I want to be made whole. Break through every layer of pride, fear, and self-preservation. Realign my heart with Yours. Restore the fear of the Lord in me. Burn away everything in me that resists You. I don't just want forgiveness—I want transformation. Thank You, Father, for not walking away. Thank You for confronting me in love, for offering realignment when I deserved rejection. Thank You for mercy that restores, for grace that redeems, and for truth that sets me free. I surrender again—with full gratitude and deep reverence. In Jesus' name. Amen.

Chapter 5

Don't Fight the Process!

If I told you I enjoyed every moment of this process, I'd be lying. There were days I thought, *"This might just finish me!"* and my prayer point became, *"God, abeg!"* (for my non-Nigerian friends, that means "God, please!"). Some moments felt like they were simply too much to carry. But here's the truth—God helped me. And what He taught me in that season can strengthen you in whatever process you're facing—or maybe avoiding—because it feels overwhelming. God's process is rarely only about punishment. It's His divine pathway to growth, transformation, and restoration. Wise leaders don't resist it—they embrace it, trusting that it heals, refines, and prepares them for greater service. In this chapter, we'll walk through the story of Naaman and draw out powerful truths about how God leads us through a divine process—not to shame us, but to shape us for something far greater.

The Law of Humility

To understand Naaman's story, we must first recognise the existence of spiritual laws, which are just as real and consequential as natural laws like gravity. One of the most vital and foundational spiritual laws is the law of humility: "*Whoever exalts himself will be humbled, and whoever humbles himself will be exalted.*"—Matthew 23:12

Jesus repeats this principle in Luke 14:11 and 18:14, highlighting its non-negotiable nature in the Kingdom of God. This isn't a poetic metaphor—it's a spiritual law with real outcomes. Just as violating the law of gravity results in falling, violating the law of humility leads to a fall in life and leadership. Humility is not an emotion—it's a decision. An attitude. It is the deliberate act of submitting our will to God. It means laying down our pride, rights, and preferences in exchange for God's will and direction. Scripture consistently teaches that those who humble themselves receive grace—and not just for forgiveness, but for progress, transformation, and blessing. "God resists the proud but gives grace to the humble."—James 4:6. Grace is God's empowerment to become what we cannot become on our own. It's the fuel for spiritual growth. Without humility, that grace is inaccessible. But when we walk in humility, we position ourselves to receive divine help—not only for healing, but for elevation, development, spiritual progress and lasting impact.

Naaman's story shows us that humility is the key to making progress in God's process. He could not be restored until he submitted. In the same way, every breakthrough we seek—whether healing, direction, deliverance, or promotion—begins with this law. If we do not humble ourselves, the process will feel like punishment, or we will not progress at all. But when we surrender with humility, we will discover that the process is actually God's pathway to promotion. Let this truth shape the way you walk through your own contradictions and seasons of transition. Humility opens the door to God's process, and His process always leads to transformation.

Contradictions in Leadership

"*Naaman, commander of the army of the king of Syria, was a great man with his master and in high favour…He was a mighty man of valour, but he was a leper.*"—2 Kings 5:1

This verse introduces us to Naaman, a highly respected and accomplished military leader. He was a national hero in Syria—favoured by his king, celebrated for his victories, and honoured as a man of valour. His name in Hebrew means pleasantness, suggesting a personality or presence that left a positive impression. But then the contradiction appears: "but he was a leper." Despite all his success, esteem, and strength, Naaman carried a condition that made him ritually and socially unclean by Israelite standards (see Leviticus 13–14; Numbers 12:1–15). His outer achievements masked an inner affliction.

In the Ancient Near East, it was common to attribute military victories to the favour of local deities. Yet Scripture makes it clear: it was the God of Israel who gave Syria victory over Israel at Ramoth-Gilead (1 Kings 22:29–36)—and He did it through the hand of this very man, Naaman. This highlights an important tension: God was using a man who, by Israelite standards, was both an outsider and ceremonially unclean. This is the paradox of Naaman's leadership—and it's one many of us can relate to.

Living With Contradictions

Naaman's life reveals what many leaders silently experience: the reality of contradiction. A contradiction is a situation where opposing truths or conditions coexist. It's being both strong and weak, elevated and broken, visible and hidden—all at the same time.

How many of us are navigating contradictions right now?

- You pray for others to be healed but privately endure chronic illness.
- You preach deliverance yet still wrestle with areas of bondage.
- You declare God as your provider, but you're clinging to Him in your own financial crisis.
- You lead people to wholeness but feel emotionally fragmented inside.

These contradictions do not make us hypocrites; they make us human. And more importantly, they position us for God's grace—if we are willing to acknowledge them and submit to His process. Naaman's contradiction was not a license for compromise. It was an invitation into transformation. His story is not to be used as an excuse to remain stuck, but as a prophetic model of God's redemptive wisdom. It teaches us that God does not despise our contradictions—He uses them to humble us, shape us, and ultimately restore us.

Contradiction is not the end—it's a catalyst. Naaman didn't let his contradiction define him, nor did he let it stop him from pursuing healing. And that's where transformation begins. Our contradictions—when surrendered to God—become the very ground where humility grows and grace flows.

Contradiction is not your disqualification; it's your invitation. If you're willing to go through the process like Naaman—with humility and faith—God can bring about complete and lasting restoration. Not just to what you do, but to who you are. You may be someone who has received prophetic words about your future—promises of leadership, business, marriage, influence, breakthrough, or impact. But while prophecy reveals destination, process is God's method of preparation. God is not just interested in getting you to the promise; He's committed to growing you into the kind of person who can sustain it.

God uses process to shape the character needed to carry the calling. And often, it's in the place of contradiction—where strengths and struggles collide—that He does His deepest work. You may feel like your current season doesn't match your prophetic promise, but this gap is not a sign that God has forgotten you. It's proof that He's forming you. So don't hide your contradiction. Don't resent the process. Bring it to the feet of the Master. Because what seems like a source of shame may be the very space where God's glory is preparing to break through. Let the contradiction push you closer to Christ. Let the process purify what pride would try to preserve. And trust that what God promised, He is faithful to perform—in His time, and through His way.

Only God Can Do This: Recognising Your Limitations

After Naaman learns that a prophet in Israel could potentially cure his leprosy, the king of Syria sends a letter to the king of Israel, along with an extravagant gift—equivalent to the annual wages of about 600 labourers. This gesture shows Naaman's desperation and his assumption that healing could be bought or negotiated through political and material means. However, the tension between Israel and Syria is so high that the king of Israel interprets the letter as a provocation—possibly an attempt to start a conflict. He tears his clothes in distress, exclaiming, "Am I God, to kill and make alive?" (2 Kings 5:7). In other words, the king recognises that what is being asked of him is impossible without divine intervention. This moment reveals something powerful: there are some healings, some deliverances, and some restorations that no human hand, influence, or wealth can accomplish. There are breakthroughs in your life that will not come by strategy, status, or connections—but only by God. Naaman begins his journey thinking that influence, position, or payment could secure his miracle. But as the story unfolds, he—like us—must come to a sobering and freeing revelation: only God can do what only God can do.

Let Go of Your Expectations: Surrender Your Presuppositions

When Naaman arrived at Elisha's house, he came with expectations. He expected a grand welcome, personal attention, and a dramatic healing. But instead, Elisha didn't even come to the door. Instead, he sent a messenger with a simple, specific instruction: "Go and wash in the Jordan seven times." (2 Kings 5:10). Naaman was offended-not just by the lack of honour he thought he deserved, but by the simplicity and location of the command. Surely, the prophet should have performed some elaborate ritual! Surely, there were better, more impressive rivers back home than the muddy Jordan! But here's the issue: Naaman's expectations nearly robbed him of his restoration. And we must ask ourselves: Are our presumptions about how God should move standing in the way of how He actually wants to move? Sometimes, like Naaman, we want divine intervention on our terms. We want the miracle but resist God's method. We expect a tailored breakthrough, forgetting that God doesn't conform to our expectations-He works according to His eternal principles.

We can get frustrated, even spiritual about it - "binding" and "casting out" things that are actually part of God's ordained processes for our progress, growth and transformation. But no amount of spiritual theatrics can override a clear instruction or God ordained process. Let this sink in: You can't cast out a process. You can only submit to it. Naaman struggled because his position, influence, and pride were clashing with God's requirement of humility and obedience. But sometimes, true deliverance demands that we choose between dignity and freedom. Will we protect our image, or pursue our healing?

The instruction was clear: "Go and wash in the Jordan." The Jordan River-156 miles long, muddy, unimpressive was not a place of glory. But that's the point. In Hebrew, Jordan means "the low place." And the low place is where God often chooses to work His greatest miracles. Let's not underestimate our low places. That's often where heaven touches earth.

Throughout Scripture, the Jordan holds prophetic significance:

- Jacob wrestled with God near its river and was transformed from deceiver to patriarch.
- Joshua led Israel through the Jordan into the Promised Land.
- Elijah was taken up in a whirlwind from the Jordan's edge.
- Jesus was baptised there, and the heavens opened.

God moves in the low place—that sacred space where identity is refined, destiny is revealed, and true power is released. I've had to walk through some really low places before. I've endured tough seasons where I was deeply misunderstood, mistreated, where relationships I had poured into shifted overnight, publicly misrepresented, painted in a way that didn't reflect the truth and stripped of direction. Yet in that low place, God met me - and He didn't come quietly. I watched God turn what looked like my breaking point into my birthing point. He gave me a joy hell couldn't steal, security no title or platform could give, a peace no man could manufacture, and a vision no betrayal could bury. What I once called an ending, Heaven had already marked as a beginning—a launchpad for healing, wholeness, and a higher call. I won't pretend the process was easy. It was hard and I didn't agree with how some things unfolded—but even in that, God was at work. Even in the mishandling, God was able to bring about deep transformation. God didn't move because some people handled me well—He moved in spite of how some people didn't. That's the mercy of God: He doesn't wait for perfect circumstances to begin His perfect work.

Even good things—like our own expectations—can distract us from the process God is calling us into. Sometimes, it's not the enemy but our own assumptions about how things should go that rob us of what God is really trying to do. I lost dignity in a moment—but I gained something far greater. And I've learned this: your lowest place can become your launching pad—if you surrender your expectations and trust God's process.

Dip 7 Times - Complete the Process!

In 2 Kings 5:10, Elisha gives Naaman a specific instruction: "*Go and wash in the Jordan seven times, and your flesh shall be restored, and you shall be clean.*" It's vital to emphasise that Naaman's restoration required more than just going to the Jordan-it required him to wash seven times. The number seven in biblical numerology represents fullness, completion, and perfection. There is a consistent pattern throughout Scripture where seven marks the completion of a divine process:

- Jacob bowed to Esau seven times-a symbol of full repentance and reconciliation (Genesis 33:3).
- On the Day of Atonement, the high priest would sprinkle the blood seven times-a symbol of complete cleansing from sin (Leviticus 16:14-17).
- Joshua and Israel circled Jericho seven times before the walls fell-representing perfect obedience (Joshua 6:4-15).
- Elijah prayed seven times before rain returned-showing full surrender and persistence (1 Kings 18:43).
- The furnace was heated seven times hotter for the three Hebrew boys-signifying the full extent of persecution and God's preserving power (Daniel 3:19).

Naaman’s sevenfold washing carries deep prophetic weight: it’s not enough to reach the low place (Jordan) — you must stay there until the process is complete. Too often, leaders want the miracle without the method, the elevation without the endurance. But there are no shortcuts in the kingdom of God. Four months into my sabbatical, I had already turned down invitations, choosing to prioritise healing and restoration. By then, I’d made meaningful progress — two therapists, weekly sessions, deep inner work, and breakthroughs in areas of past trauma. I genuinely felt peace and thought, “Maybe it’s time to step out again.” Invitations were waiting, including some international ones, and I felt ready to re-engage. But when I sought wisdom from my mentor, Dr. Sharon, she gave counsel I didn’t expect: “Take a bit more time. Not as punishment, but to allow for full restoration." Looking back, I'm so glad I listened. I had been used to recovering just enough to keep functioning, but that extra time rooted me deeper — beyond self-effort or the need to promote myself — into the confidence of God's promotion. As pastors and leaders, we can receive just enough healing to operate — but not enough to truly transform. And it's transformation, not mere functionality, that sustains long-term fruitfulness. Whatever it looks like for you — take the time. Take a sabbatical. Seek therapy. Submit to your leader. Fast and pray. Get deliverance. Sit with your spouse and children and be restored together. Don't cut corners. Don't settle for partial healing. Complete the process.

Restoration: The Fruit of God's Process

The story concludes in 2 Kings 5:14: "*So he went down and dipped himself seven times in the Jordan, according to the word of the man of God, and his flesh was restored like the flesh of a little child, and he was clean.*"

Restoration can be defined as "the action of returning something to a former owner, place, or condition." Naaman's choice to submit to God's universal law of humility positioned him for deliverance, restoration, and divine progress. The same is true for us: when we humble ourselves and yield to God's process, transformation follows. I've lived this. I walked through a season that felt like everything was being stripped away. It was painful, dark, and deeply disorienting. Yet in that place, God began to reveal things I could never have seen from a posture of strength alone. There are perspectives, healing, and clarity that only humility can unlock.

This isn't wishful thinking or a fairytale—it's my reality. In less than a year, I watched God swing open doors I never knocked on, release financial favour I couldn't have earned, and breathe life into relationships I thought were gone forever—while bringing new ones that carried greater depth and purpose than I'd ever imagined. What I received far outweighed what I lost. And it didn't happen because I chased it—it happened because I surrendered to the process. So, let me ask you: what process is God calling you into right now? Is it in your business? Your relationships? Your leadership? Don't fight it. Don't shortcut it. The other side of obedience is not just survival—it's growth, transformation, progress, and breakthrough.

<u>Chapter 5 Reflections: Don't Fight the Process!</u>

Memory Verse

"Whoever exalts himself will be humbled, and whoever humbles himself will be exalted."-Matthew 23:12

"So he went down and dipped himself seven times in the Jordan, according to the word of the man of God, and his flesh was restored like the flesh of a little child, and he was clean."-2 Kings 5:14

<u>Personal Reflective Questions</u>

1. <u>Where in my life is God calling me to embrace the law of humility?</u>
   - Am I surrendering to His will, or still trying to maintain control or image?
2. <u>Have I been viewing God's process as punishment instead of preparation?</u>
   - How would my attitude change if I saw the process as a gift of grace?
3. <u>What contradictions in my life reveal the need for deeper dependence on God?</u>
   - Have I let my strength mask the areas where I still need healing?
4. <u>Am I willing to obey God's simple instruction, even if it seems beneath me or unexpected?</u>
   - Like Naaman, am I offended by the method and missing the miracle?

5. What would it look like for me to 'dip seven times'?

- What does full obedience and complete surrender look like in this season?

6. In what area is God inviting me to trust His promotion rather than seek my own?

- How can I choose humility today in my business, family, or leadership?

Closing Prayer

Father, I thank You for the law of humility-that when I humble myself, You give grace and lift me up in due time. Forgive me for the times I've resisted Your process or tried to preserve my pride. Today, I surrender fully. I lay down my expectations, my assumptions, and my need for control. Teach me to embrace the low place, where You do Your greatest work. Like Naaman, I choose to obey-even when I don't understand. I trust Your methods, Your timing, and Your heart. Complete the work You've started in me. Restore me not just in appearance, but in identity, purpose, and wholeness. I declare that on the other side of humility is healing, breakthrough, and elevation. In Jesus' name, amen.

Chapter 6

Alignment for Assignment: Breaking Demonic Soul Ties

The Power of Honest Reflection

There are moments in life and ministry when the noise must stop—when the demands, the platforms, and the expectations must quiet down so you can truly hear your own soul. That's what this season gave me. Space to ask myself some deeper questions—without the pressure to perform, without any distractions, without minimising my feelings, and without pretending I was fine. How had my relationship with my father influenced how I see God? When I was told my cousin's life was taken, how did that shape my view of justice? Did it leave unprocessed grief or stir a desire for justice I hadn't yet surrendered to God? Had I, in some areas of life, traded away part of my value for the approval of others? I had to ask these questions with brutal honesty, especially as I reflected on how I've navigated friendships and past relationships. Were my choices shaped by security and God-given identity—or by fear of rejection, people pleasing and the need to be needed? The answers weren't all easy to hear. Some made me laugh. Some made me sigh. Others brought tears. Others brought anger. But most of all, they brought clarity—a holy awareness of where I was in those past moments, how I'd arrived there, and who God was calling me to become. This wasn't a one-time reflection; these are questions I revisit regularly as a leader. But in this season of intentional stillness and real rest, I could see Satan's traps with sharper vision; the subtle lies I had tolerated, the patterns I had excused, and the compromises I had justified. Without distraction, I could address them—not in shame, but with grace and Spirit-led strategic prayer. That stillness and confrontation brought undeniable alignment for my assignment. It reminded me that wholeness is a non-negotiable for anyone who wants to fulfil their God given assignment. That's the heartbeat of this chapter.

You cannot walk fully in your divine assignment without being properly aligned. God designed soul ties as spiritual channels for love, growth, and mission. However, when these alignments are perverted or mismanaged, they become demonic soul ties—hindrances that entangle the soul and delay destiny. Breaking ungodly soul ties is a necessary spiritual act to realign with God's purpose and walk in true freedom. From the beginning, God created us for alignment—divinely ordered relationships through which His love, power, and purposes flow. These connections, called soul ties, serve as spiritual bridges between people, modelling the intimacy God desires with us. Whether in marriage, family, friendship, or the Church, these God-ordained bonds shape our minds, influence our decisions, and affect our spiritual trajectory.

However, not all soul ties are holy. Satan cannot create, only pervert. The enemy's tactic is to distort what God designs—turning soul ties meant for life into entanglements that breed fear, control, lust, or spiritual decay. These demonic soul ties form through unhealthy relationships, unrepented sin, trauma, and idolatrous spiritual activity. Left unbroken, they act as spiritual baggage that weighs us down, stifling intimacy with God and blocking our ability to fulfil His assignment. To step into your divine assignment, you must first examine your alignments. Who has access to your soul? What voices shape your inner world? Are your relationships channels of God's grace—or open doors for oppression and delay?

In this chapter, we will explore:

- The benefits of godly soul ties and how they align us with God's will.
- The types of soul ties and their spiritual function.
- How demonic soul ties form, often subtly but with serious consequences.
- How to identify, confront, and break these ties through repentance and spiritual warfare.

This chapter is not just about deliverance—it's about freedom, clarity, and reclaiming the authority to walk in your assignment. As you learn to discern the soul ties influencing your life, you will gain power to break what binds and build what blesses.

What Is a Soul Tie?

God created humanity for relationship—first with Himself and then with others. A soul tie is a spiritual and emotional bond between two or more people, designed by God and founded upon love, unity, and purpose. These God-ordained relationships form alignments, which are critical for spiritual growth and destiny. A godly soul tie functions as a spiritual channel, allowing the Holy Spirit to move and influence individuals through the bond they share. Through these connections, God imparts wisdom, character, support, and spiritual insight.

Why Godly Soul Ties Matter

God uses soul ties to:

- Reflect His nature through human relationships.
- Help us understand spiritual truths by experiencing them naturally.
- Equip us for His assignment through divine alignment.

When soul ties are formed according to God's will, they become a powerful tool for spiritual growth, emotional health, and Kingdom impact.

Types of Soul Ties

Godly soul ties reflect the divine blueprint for relationships. Each type models a unique spiritual truth, showing how human connection—when submitted to God—can become a channel of divine influence.

1. Marriage

Key Scriptures: Genesis 2:24, Matthew 19:6

The Hebrew word for "cleave" (dabaq) means "to weld" or "to glue," indicating a powerful, enduring bond. In marriage, this soul tie is forged through covenant and love. It may involve pain, not from manipulation, but from the deep merging of two distinct souls into "one flesh." When such a relationship is severed, the pain of loss stems from a part of your soul remaining with the other. This depth of union reflects Christ's love for the Church—sacrificial, unifying, and eternal.

2. Friendship

Key Scripture: 1 Samuel 18:1–2

The bond between David and Jonathan is described with the same Hebrew term as in marriage: knit (dabaq). This shows that soul ties formed in friendship can be just as spiritually powerful. Godly friendship is selfless and mutually protective. Each person genuinely seeks the other's well-being, making the relationship a reflection of Christ's love and character.

3. Parents and Children

Key Scripture: Genesis 44:30

A parental soul tie forms from birth—spiritually, emotionally, and neurologically. This connection influences thought patterns and emotional health, creating a powerful spiritual channel between parent and child. In Genesis 44, Judah pleads with Joseph for Benjamin's release, expressing how deeply their father Jacob's soul is tied to his son. Jacob's despair over Joseph's presumed death (Genesis 37) shows the intensity of a parental soul tie—so deep that emotional trauma can impact the soul's vitality. This aligns with attachment theory in social work, where early bonds influence lifelong relational patterns. A godly parental tie brings nurture, identity, and healthy emotional development.

4. The Church (Body of Christ)

Key Scriptures: Ephesians 4:16, 2 Peter 1:1

The Church is not merely an institution but a living Body, joined together both physically and spiritually. The Greek term for “joined” in Ephesians 4:16 shares the same root as “cleave” in Genesis 2:24.

True unity in the Body of Christ comes not from uniformity but from shared faith, purpose, and spiritual intimacy. Through love and mutual submission, believers grow together in Christ. When properly stewarded, this soul tie strengthens our walk, matures our character, and protects us from isolation. Note: When we draw close to Christ, we naturally grow closer to others who are also walking with Him. Every deposit of God in a believer is meant to edify and influence others in the Body of Christ.

5. God (Our Creator and Father)

Key Scripture: Deuteronomy 11:22

The very first soul tie ever formed was between God and man. In Deuteronomy 11:22, God commands His people to “hold fast” to Him. The term “hold fast” (dabaq) again implies the welding of souls—complete union. God’s greatest desire is to dwell in us, not just with us. The highest form of intimacy is shared life. A soul tie with the Lord is the foundation of all other relationships—it defines our identity, shapes our destiny, and secures our eternity.

Closing Thought:

Each godly soul tie represents a spiritual bridge—a relational pathway through which God imparts purpose, protection, and growth. Whether in marriage, friendship, family, the Church, or directly with the Lord, these ties are sacred. They must be discerned, protected, and cherished.

What Is a Demonic Soul Tie?

Satan does not create; he only perverts what God has made. Every godly design can be distorted when misused or mishandled—including relationships. A demonic soul tie is the perversion of a soul tie originally designed by God for love, growth, and divine alignment.

Definition:

A demonic soul tie is a spiritual bond between two or more people, established not on God's love or truth, but on lust, fear, manipulation, trauma, or any of the works of the flesh listed in Galatians 5:19–21. These perverted alignments open spiritual channels for demonic influence, oppression and control.

How Demonic Soul Ties Form

Satan's primary strategy to stop your assignment is to pervert your alignment.

Godly soul ties are meant to direct you toward your destiny. When alignment is compromised, it becomes a doorway rather than a bridge—a gateway for demonic influence.

1. Sexual Sin

Scripture Reference: 1 Corinthians 6:16 "*Or do you not know that he who is joined to a prostitute becomes one body with her? For, as it is written, 'The two will become one flesh*'". Sexual intimacy was created to seal covenant and form a godly soul tie within marriage. When this is practised outside of God's covenant—whether through fornication, adultery, pornography, or prostitution—it forms a perverted soul tie.

The soul does not differentiate between a covenant marriage and a casual hookup. It still joins. These soul ties open the door for demonic access, leading to:

- Obsession or emotional entanglement
- Sexual confusion or perversion
- Emotional instability
- Repeated cycles of lust, fear and brokenness

When a soul tie is created through sexual sin, the spiritual baggage is not left behind after the act ends. Instead, it is carried forward, affecting every future relationship, your sense of self, and your ability to walk in purity and clarity.

2. Dysfunctional Friendships: When Brokenness Binds

Not every dysfunction in your life was taught—some things were transferred. We often become who we are not just through intentional teaching, but through spiritual influence. This is especially true in the context of friendships, where unspoken patterns, emotional dependencies, and spiritual alignments shape who we become—sometimes more than we realise.

The Foundation of Dysfunctional Friendships

In a dysfunctional friendship, your brokenness becomes the glue. These friendships are not built on mutual growth, respect, or purpose—but on shared wounds, insecurities, mutual need or mutual enemies.

- Dysfunction becomes the currency of the connection.
- You stay close not because of destiny but because of *co-dependency*.

- Instead of sharpening each other, you *soothe* each other's sin.

When you constantly find yourself drained, anxious, or compromising in a friendship, it may not be God-ordained—it may be soul-entangling.

Rejection Opens Doors

One of the hidden roots of dysfunctional friendships is the spirit of rejection. When rejection is at work, love is treated like a reward instead of a foundation. People begin to withdraw affection or attention in subtle ways to *control you emotionally*. This manipulative pattern causes you to overextend yourself in the name of "love." When you are a loving person, your first instinct is to give more. But the enemy knows this—and uses your love to manipulate you into bondage. You end up performing for approval instead of living from acceptance.

Whose Approval Are You Chasing?

When we pursue people's approval over God's, we've unknowingly opened a spiritual door to demonic influence. *"For am I now seeking the approval of man, or of God?"* – Galatians 1:10. The spirit of rejection uses your desire for love and connection to redirect your loyalty away from God and toward dysfunctional people. This is how soul ties form in friendships—not just through deep affection, but through emotional leverage.

What Is a Friend, Really?

One of the definitions of the word *friend* is "one who loves."

So the real question you must ask is:

- Is this truly love?
- Is this person pushing you closer to God or further from your identity in Him?
- Are they celebrating your growth or competing with your healing?
- Are they present when you have nothing to offer?

If love is only available when you're useful, that's not friendship—it's bondage. Godly friendships will refine your soul. Dysfunctional friendships will drain your spirit. You cannot walk in your God-given identity while staying tied to people who benefit from your brokenness. To protect your purpose, you must discern your alignments. "Do not be misled: 'Bad company corrupts good character.'" – 1 Corinthians 15:33

3. Demonic Soul Ties in Parent-Child Relationships

Not all soul ties are birthed through romance or friendship—some of the most spiritually impactful ties are formed (or perverted) in family dynamics, especially between parents and children. "*For this reason, a man shall leave his father and mother and be joined to his wife...*" — Ephesians 5:31.

This passage reflects a spiritual principle: the necessity of leaving in order to cleave. And it's more than physical—it's emotional, spiritual, and psychological.

The Transfer of Spiritual Authority

One of the most sacred moments in a traditional wedding ceremony is when the officiant asks: "Who gives this woman to be married to this man?"

In this moment, the father steps forward—not only giving his daughter in marriage but also relinquishing spiritual authority. He is saying: "I now recognise that a new spiritual headship is forming. My daughter is no longer under my covering in the same way." This release is not rejection, but realignment. A healthy father-daughter soul tie is being redefined, not destroyed. The father is saying, spiritually: "I step back so this new covenant can flourish."

When Parental Soul Ties Are Not Released

However, when this spiritual transition does not occur, or worse, when parents operate under a controlling or rejection-based spirit, the relationship can be perverted and become a demonic soul tie.

In these cases:

- The parent refuses to allow the child to mature, make decisions, or establish boundaries.
- Love becomes conditional.
- Affection is withheld to punish or manipulate.
- The child's life is lived for parental approval or out of fear of disappointment.

This is not nurturing—this is spiritual bondage. Even among unmarried people, this can manifest when a parent remains an unhealthy influence, preventing their child from stepping into God-given purpose or identity. Control disguised as "care" becomes witchcraft when it overrides the will of another.

Spiritual & Psychological Impact

In Jewish tradition, although a son may remain physically in the home, he spiritually leaves the authority of his parents to cleave to his wife. This leaving is not abandonment—it's repositioning. The husband becomes not just a lover, but a source and covering, like a father to his bride in terms of spiritual leadership.

If this transition is blocked, the result is:

- Over-involved parents.
- Spouses who are emotionally still children.
- Adults who cannot function without parental input or permission.

Demonic Soul Ties Can Form from Absence Too

It's not only perversion that opens the door—it can also be neglect or absence. In social work, children with emotionally or physically absent parents often struggle with:

- Identity confusion
- Emotional dysregulation
- Attachment disorders

These unmet needs create a void—and voids become doorways. We were created for godly bonds, so when those are absent, we instinctively reach for replacements, healthy or unhealthy. This is where demonic soul ties can take root—through unhealthy coping mechanisms like:

- Sexual promiscuity
- Co-dependency or independence
- Addiction
- Performance-driven self-worth

The unmet need becomes an idol, and what was once a cry for connection becomes a contract with dysfunction.

Parental Influence Affects Your View of God

Perhaps the most sobering reality is this:

A distorted view of your earthly parents can imprint a distorted view of God the Father.

If a parent was abusive, absent, controlling, or inconsistent, it can create a false soul tie that blocks intimacy with God. Instead of running to Him, we may flinch, avoid, or perform—because our spirit still remembers the pain of our first alignment. This is not just a psychological wound—it's a spiritual entanglement.

4. Demonic Soul Ties in the Church

"*But God has composed the body... that there should be no division in the body, but that the members should have the same care for one another.*" — 1 Corinthians 12:24–25

God designed the Church for unity, healing, and growth—a place where believers are joined together in like precious faith (2 Peter 1:1). The soul ties in the Body of Christ are meant to be godly, built on love, mutual submission, and spiritual alignment. But where God plants unity, Satan seeks to sow division.

Satanic Strategy: Perverting Unity into Cliques

One of the ways the enemy infiltrates the Church is by perverting godly soul ties into demonic alliances, such as cliques and exclusive circles.

A clique is not just a group of close friends; it becomes demonic when:

- It excludes others intentionally.
- It creates division in the church body.
- It prioritises loyalty to people over loyalty to the Spirit of God.

These kinds of soul ties feed off pride, favouritism, and fear of rejection, not love. What was meant to foster edification turns into a channel for demonic influence. Any relationship that comes against the general unity God is trying to reproduce is demonic.

Unforgiveness: A Demonic Wedge in the Body

Unforgiveness is another key way Satan manipulates godly bonds. A godly soul tie is meant to carry love, mercy, and restoration—but when bitterness and offence take root, the tie becomes toxic. Unforgiveness is the perversion of a godly soul tie. It causes emotional and spiritual separation within the Body. It prevents believers from walking in the fullness of their assignments. "*Be kind to one another, tender-hearted, forgiving one another, as God in Christ forgave you.*" — Ephesians 4:32

Satan's goal is not just to wound you but to weaponise your pain so that your heart is hardened against your brother or sister in Christ. He knows that if enough members of the Body of Christ become offended, he can infest the Church with division.

Soul Ties & Groupthink

Demonic soul ties can also lead to spiritual manipulation, where the opinions of a few overrides the discernment of the Holy Spirit.

This can manifest as:

- Groupthink: where the clique's beliefs or values dominate the culture of the church.
- Manipulation: loyalty to the group becomes more important than loyalty to Christ.
- Control: members fear rejection or isolation if they question or confront wrong behaviour.

This behaviour grieves the Holy Spirit and blocks the corporate flow of revelation, healing, and growth in the Church.

5. Demonic Soul Ties through Foreign Spiritual Engagement

"*You cannot drink the cup of the Lord and the cup of demons too; you cannot have a part in both the Lord's table and the table of demons.*"— 1 Corinthians 10:21

When we give ourselves to Christ, we are spiritually joined to Him (1 Corinthians 6:17). He becomes our source of truth, identity, and direction. But any spiritual engagement outside of Christ is not neutral—it creates demonic soul ties.

Spiritual Infidelity Forms Demonic Bonds

When someone participates in spiritual practices outside of God—such as:

- Consulting mediums, horoscopes, or psychics
- Engaging in occult rituals or witchcraft
- Seeking healing, direction, or protection through New Age or ancestral practices

They are not just exploring "alternative" options—they are joining themselves to another spirit. "Their idols are silver and gold, the work of human hands. They have mouths, but do not speak; eyes, but do not see… those who make them become like them, so do all who trust in them." — Psalm 115:4–8. Just as we are joined to Christ in covenant, engaging with spiritual forces not rooted in Christ creates a counterfeit covenant—a demonic soul tie that opens spiritual channels for deception, oppression, and bondage.

Spiritual Senses Become Dull and Darkened

God gave us spiritual faculties to engage with Him:

- Eyes to see Him
- Ears to hear Him
- A Heart to engage Him
- Hands to touch and minister
- Feet to walk in purpose

But when we engage with unauthorised spiritual forces, these faculties become corrupted. Our sight is blurred, hearing is distorted, and our spiritual discernment begins to decay. We become like what we worship—powerless, blind, deaf, and mute in the spirit (Psalm 115:8). Demonic soul ties numb our sensitivity to the Holy Spirit and hinder our ability to operate in our spiritual assignments.

6. Demonic Soul Ties Through Bereavement

Grief is a natural response to loss. God allows space for mourning—He Himself is close to the broken-hearted (Psalm 34:18). Jesus Himself wept at the tomb of Lazarus (John 11:35). Mourning is not sinful—it is necessary. In fact, in the Old Testament, there were set times of mourning (Genesis 50:10; Deuteronomy 34:8), which helped people acknowledge loss while still transitioning back into purpose. But Satan, the master of perversion, often uses bereavement as a strategic entry point to form demonic soul ties.

When Grief Becomes a Stronghold

A demonic soul tie through bereavement happens when grief moves from a season into a spiritual stronghold. Instead of processing loss and moving forward with the assignment of God, the individual becomes spiritually tied to the deceased or to the pain of their absence.

This may manifest in:

- Prolonged or unresolved grief
- Fixation on the dead beyond remembrance (idolatry of memory)
- Withdrawing from purpose, relationships, and joy
- Bitterness or anger toward God

The enemy uses this to arrest a person's spiritual momentum, tying them to the past and choking their present assignment.

Grief Becomes a Soul Tie When:

- A person cannot emotionally detach from the deceased, even after time and prayer
- The identity of the individual becomes permanently wrapped in their loss
- There's a deep inner vow like, "I'll never recover from this", "I died when they died"
- The memory becomes a spiritual idol, affecting choices, relationships, or obedience
- Attraction to the occult or seeking mediums to contact the dead (Leviticus 19:31).

In these cases, the soul is not only mourning but bound, and that bond must be broken.

God's Remedy: Grieve with Hope

"*We do not grieve like the rest of mankind, who have no hope.*" — 1 Thessalonians 4:13.

The hope of the believer is that death is not the end. Jesus conquered death, and in Him, we live again. The enemy wants to use the pain of separation to separate us from our purpose.

But God calls us to:

- Mourn, but not remain in mourning.
- Release the person to God—not forget but detach the soul tie.
- Pick up the baton and continue the race marked out for us (Hebrews 12:1).
- Trust God's timing and sovereignty even in loss.

Breaking the Soul Tie of Bereavement

- Acknowledge the grief and the soul tie – Admit that your soul is still entangled in a way that hinders your assignment.
- Repent of anything that has become idolatrous – memories, inner vows, or anger at God.
- Renounce the soul tie – Break any inner agreements like "I can't live without them."
- Receive healing and new purpose – Isaiah 61:3 says He gives "a garment of praise instead of a spirit of heaviness."
- Move forward intentionally – Ask God to restore your sense of direction and joy.

Testimony: "That Friday Changed Everything"

I can never forget that Friday. Four days after learning of my father's passing, our family was hit with another devastating blow: news came that my cousin's life had been violently taken. It was grief upon grief—loss layered on loss. I had no frame of reference for that kind of pain. The shock was overwhelming, the weight crushing. I knew I needed space to process my father passing, but the grief felt like too much to carry all at once. My therapist once shared how a seemingly small event had unexpectedly triggered emotions buried from much earlier seasons of his life. It helped me understand something crucial: not all grief shows up in the moment. Some wounds surface later, when something else awakens what's been buried. It took me years to realise I was still carrying unprocessed pain that the enemy was trying to use against me. During my sabbatical, I decided to be intentional. I cleared space—no noise, no distractions—and set aside time for prayer and fasting. I came before God with an open heart, asking Him to reveal and heal every hidden place. In a series of visions, He showed me countless people who would one day walk in freedom because of my testimony. In His presence, I released and renounced the things Satan was trying to use to entrap my soul and hinder my alignments:

- The rejection I had internalised from different seasons of life, relationships and ministry.
- The unforgiveness trying to take root from moments of injustice and betrayal.
- The fear of future pain.
- The compounded weight of past trauma I hadn't fully faced.

And let me tell you—God met me there. The false identities and labels that sought to redefine me through past mistakes, sin, trauma or compromise—could not stand against the truth of who God says I am.

- There was healing.
- There was restoration.
- There was breaking and there was release.

God is not just the God who saves—He is the God who heals the soul and restores what was stolen. This is not just my story—it can be yours too. You might be sitting here today thinking, "I've moved on," But some of us have survived seasons that we've never actually healed from. And I came to tell you today: God will do it for you too. "He heals the broken-hearted and binds up their wounds." —Psalm 147:3. If you're ready, God is waiting. He is ready to sever every demonic soul tie formed through trauma, grief, fear, and false alignment. He is ready to heal the places you didn't even know were broken. He is ready to restore your identity, your joy, and your freedom. All He needs is your yes. Are you ready to engage in repentance and spiritual warfare? Are you ready for God to restore you?

How to Break Demonic Soul Ties

1. Repentance & Renouncement – Turning and Disconnecting

Repentance means turning from sin and returning to God, but it must be followed by renunciation, which is how we cancel legal rights the enemy may have gained. Renouncement is saying "I divorce with, I no longer agree, I separate from, no longer participate in, or accept this connection in my life." As you walk through each area below, both repent (turn from) and renounce (break agreement with) the specific stronghold. Speak these out loud with faith:

A. Sexual Sin

''Father, I come before You in full surrender and humility. I repent of every sexual sin I have committed — knowingly and unknowingly — that has opened doors for demonic soul ties. I repent of fornication, adultery, pornography, masturbation, and all sexual activity outside of the covenant of marriage as You designed it. I renounce every ungodly soul tie formed through sexual sin. I break every invisible chain connecting me to past partners, encounters, and images. I command every part of my soul that was left with them to return to me now, and I release every part of them that is still tied to me. In the name of Jesus, I renounce every spirit husband and spirit wife that has laid claim to me through these soul ties, dreams, covenants, or bloodlines. I cancel every spiritual marriage made without my knowledge or through ungodly unions. I break every contract, ring, altar, or covenant that links me to demonic spouses or sexual spirits. I reject every form of night visitation, sexual dreams, manipulation, and torment. I cover myself with the blood of Jesus. I declare that my body is the temple of the Holy Spirit and no longer a dwelling place for lust, shame, or perversion. Father, cleanse my memory, my body, and my emotions. Heal every fractured part of my identity and restore my purity. I declare freedom from all shame and guilt. I reclaim my purity. I now walk in wholeness, dignity, holiness and kingdom alignment by the power of the Holy Spirit in Jesus' name. Amen."

B. Dysfunctional Friendships

"Father, I repent of every friendship I remained in that was built on rejection, control, gossip, insecurity, comparison, or fear of man. I've placed people's opinions above Your voice and compromised my calling for connection. I renounce every emotional or spiritual tie formed through these unhealthy friendships. I come out of agreement with every identity shaped by other people's dysfunction. I break all manipulation and soul-dependence that hindered my maturity. In the name of Jesus, I cut off every tie that drains my joy, peace, and purpose. I receive Your love and validation. I will build relationships on truth, honour, and mutual freedom, not co-dependency in Jesus' name. Amen."

C. Church Cliques / Offence in the Body of Christ

"Lord, I repent for allowing offence, pride, elitism, inferiority, superiority, or division to operate in my heart in the context of church relationships. I repent for forming exclusive cliques that caused division or wounded others. I renounce every soul tie formed through gossip, competition, judgement, and spiritual superiority. I come out of agreement with bitterness, spiritual hierarchy, and offence. I forgive every leader, member, or friend who hurt me — and I release myself from the prison of unforgiveness, bitterness and resentment. In Jesus' name, I break every demonic tie to conversations, groups, or ideologies that hinder the unity of the Body of Christ. I receive a fresh heart of love, unity, and humility toward Your Church. Make me a vessel of healing and reconciliation in Jesus' name. Amen."

D. Bereavement & Loss

"Father, I repent for every way I've allowed grief to define me more than Your promises. I honour the memory of my loved ones, but I repent for every place where I stayed stuck, allowing grief to override my purpose. I renounce every unhealthy attachment to those who passed away. I break ties with spirits of mourning, heaviness, and despair that have lingered beyond the season You assigned. I come out of agreement with the lie that I cannot move forward. I declare that the time to mourn has ended, and the time to rise and build has come. In Jesus' name, I sever every demonic soul tie that formed through prolonged grief, loss, or trauma. I receive the oil of joy for mourning and beauty for ashes in Jesus' name. Amen."

E. Idolatry / False Spiritual Practices

"Lord Jesus, I repent for every time I turned to spiritual practices, powers, or people outside of You — whether knowingly or unknowingly. I confess and repent for engaging with witchcraft, ancestral practices, horoscopes, crystals, talismans, rituals, New Age or any spiritual guidance apart from the Holy Spirit. I renounce all soul ties and covenants formed through those encounters. I break agreement with every foreign altar, spiritual contract, and demonic ritual I participated in. In Jesus' name, I close every door opened to the enemy and command every attached spirit to leave. I plead the blood of Jesus over my mind, my lineage, and my spiritual sensitivity. I dedicate all my spiritual senses to Christ alone — my eyes will see You, my ears will hear You, and my life will glorify You in Jesus' name. Amen."

F. Trauma

"Father, I come to You today and I repent for every way I have allowed trauma to define me more than Your truth. I repent for internalising pain, fear, anxiety, and shame instead of running to You as my refuge and healer. I renounce every soul tie formed through traumatic experiences — including abuse, neglect, violence, abandonment, betrayal, or sudden crisis. I break all ties to the moment trauma entered and I reject every false identity formed from that place. I come out of agreement with fear, hypervigilance, victimhood, despair, and mistrust. Trauma is not my home. I renounce every spirit that used trauma as a legal right to stay in my soul — including torment, fear, confusion, rejection, or self-hatred. In the name of Jesus, I command every residue of trauma to leave my mind, emotions, and memory. I declare healing over my nervous system, over my dreams, over my personality. I receive peace, restoration, and clarity. I am not second-class. I am not broken — I am being made whole by the One who heals all wounds. I choose to walk forward not in survival, but in victory in Jesus' name. Amen."

Breaking the Tie: When Testimony Unlocks Freedom

Roberta had been married for many years. Roberta and her husband had five children and were respected pillars in their community for their charitable work for the homeless. Over the years, I had spent time with them—praying, counselling, and ministering to the family. By God's grace, several people in the household came to know Christ through those encounters. During my sabbatical, I received a call from Roberta. Her sister was unwell, and she asked me to come and pray. I took it to prayer and sensed the Holy Spirit prompting me strongly to go. As I was driving, I asked the Lord what He wanted me to say or do. He began to speak clearly—He wanted me to share parts of my testimony, particularly around healing and restoration, to stir hope. When I arrived, we prayed, and God's presence filled the room. Roberta's sister, who had been bedridden, was deeply moved under the weight of the Holy Spirit and the prophetic words spoken over her. I also felt led to share directly with Roberta how God had walked me through freedom from compounded trauma, fear of abandonment, rejection, lust and shame. Those chains are no longer my reality. I made it clear this freedom was not the result of one single moment, but an ongoing walk—sustained daily through surrender to Jesus, time in His Word, and consistent dependence on the Holy Spirit. They were encouraged, and her sister even reported feeling physically better. As I made my way to the car, Roberta called out, "Can I speak to you?" I stopped. Her voice shook as she confessed, she had been in an affair for a few years. Guilt, grief, and conviction poured out as she spoke. I didn't condemn her; I listened without judgement —I then pointed her to the same Jesus who had set me free from the chains of my past. "*If He could do it for me, He can do it for you if you are willing,*" I told her. She was willing. She chose to believe it. Right there, we prayed. She repented, renounced the soul tie, and decisively ended the relationship. The journey ahead for Roberta would be about rebuilding trust and walking in healing, but that day, a spiritual turning point took place: breaking the demonic soul tie and choosing Gods way. Today, Roberta's marriage is still intact, and God is being glorified through the ongoing restoration of her home.

This experience reminded me of something profound: when we remove the log from our own eyes, we can see clearly to help others. And when we share our testimony—led by the Spirit—it doesn't just inspire. It pierces. It locates. It delivers. Even when our stories don't directly match someone's situation, the prophetic power in our transparency creates an atmosphere for The Holy Spirit to bring conviction, healing, and breakthrough.

Conclusion

Your story was never meant to remain silent. God does not waste your pain, your past, or your process. Every scar, every battle, every breakthrough carries prophetic power—not just for you, but for someone else's freedom. Just like my testimony became the key that unlocked Roberta's healing, your story is a weapon in the hands of God—sharp enough to break chains, bold enough to silence shame, and strong enough to dismantle the enemy's lies. But to walk in your assignment, you must walk free. No more baggage.

No more weight. No more soul ties holding you hostage to old seasons and false identities. By the power of the Holy Spirit, it's time to rise. Renounce every ungodly bond. Repent for every place where alignment was broken. And take your place—not as a wounded warrior, but as a restored vessel ready to do damage to the kingdom of darkness. You are free. You are chosen. You are called. Now go—walk in it!

Chapter 6 Reflection: Alignment for Assignment: Breaking Demonic Soul Ties

Memory Prompt:

Take a moment to recall a time when someone else's story deeply impacted your own journey. How did God use their testimony to bring light to a hidden area in your life? Now, consider a moment in your own life—whether painful, redemptive, or still in process—that God may want to use to set someone else free.

Personal Reflection Questions

1. Where have I seen God's restoration power in my life, even if I haven't shared it yet?
2. Are there areas in my past that I've kept silent out of fear, shame, or uncertainty?
3. Have I ever felt the Holy Spirit nudge me to share my testimony with someone, and how did I respond?
4. Who in my life may need to hear a part of my story to find hope or healing?
5. Are there ungodly soul ties (relationships, beliefs, or emotional attachments) that may still be affecting how freely I walk in my calling?
6. What would it look like for me to take my place in God's assignment without baggage, shame, or fear?
7. Have I allowed the Holy Spirit to fully heal and release me from every past tie or weight?

Closing Prayer

Father, thank You that my story is not a mistake—it's a testimony of Your power, Your grace, and Your goodness. I surrender every chapter of my past to You. Use it as a weapon in Your hands to set others free. I renounce every weight, every soul tie, and every lie that has tried to keep me silent or stuck. By the power of the Holy Spirit, I take my place—restored, bold, and ready. In Jesus' name, Amen.

Section 2 - Refined: Formed in Fire

Formation of the Leader in Practice &
Stewardship of Calling

Focus: Restoration, grace, conflict, betrayal, boundaries, and stewardship.

Chapter 7

Leading by Grace: When Mercy Offends the Religious

I will never forget one pivotal conversation I had with Dr. Ralph about showing grace in leadership. He shared stories of enduring deeply negative experiences from people in ministry—moments that would have justified harsh responses—yet, by God's grace, he was able to show love and mercy. It shook me. His ability to combine firm authority with genuine grace not only inspired me, it also gave me a living template. I began to see that grace in leadership is more than a kind gesture in the moment—it is a legacy that shapes how our leadership will be remembered tomorrow. The grace of God in leadership is both offensive and transformative—challenging religious pride while empowering leaders to lead from a place of mercy, not merit. In the economy of God's kingdom, grace is not just a gift—it is a test. While it saves, restores, and empowers, grace also offends the self-righteous, confuses the prideful, and exposes the hidden motives of leaders. True spiritual leadership requires more than charisma or competence—it demands a deep, personal response to God's grace and an equally humble posture when that grace is extended to others, especially those we deem undeserving. This chapter explores the uncomfortable, often scandalous nature of grace in the life of a leader. Using Jonah as a case study, we will examine how a prophet of God, though familiar with divine grace, struggled with its implications when it was offered beyond the boundaries of his own preferences, prejudices, and national pride. Jonah's story serves as both a warning and a mirror for leaders today. It forces us to ask: Do I truly lead from grace?

Or do I only celebrate grace when it serves my agenda? To lead by grace, we must first be transformed by grace—and that transformation is often as offensive as it is necessary.

The Grace of God

To fully grasp the leadership lessons embedded in the book of Jonah, we must begin with its central theme: the boundless compassion—or grace—of God. While the fullness of grace is revealed in the New Testament through Jesus Christ, its foundations are firmly established in the Old Testament. In Exodus 34:6, God reveals His essential character to Moses, declaring, "*The Lord, the Lord, a God merciful and gracious, slow to anger, and abounding in steadfast love and faithfulness.*" This revelation is God's response to Moses' desperate prayer in Exodus 33:18: "Show me Your glory." God answered by placing Moses in the cleft of a rock and proclaiming His gracious nature, which would become the foundation for His covenant relationship with Israel.

Grace, biblically defined, is unmerited favour—freely given, never achieved. It is the divine power that carries every dimension of our life in God. Scripture outlines several ways this grace operates in the believer's journey:

- Saved by grace – Ephesians 2:8-9
- Serve by grace – Hebrews 12:28
- Gifted by grace – Romans 12:6
- Taught to live righteously by grace – Titus 2:11-14
- Forgiven and justified by grace – Romans 3:24
- Matured by grace – 2 Peter 3:18
- Used for God's purposes by grace – Ephesians 3:7

The scene with Moses also serves as a prophetic picture of the New Covenant reality in Christ. Just as God placed Moses in the rock to reveal His glory, so too has He placed us "in Christ," the true Rock, to experience and reflect His grace and glory. It is significant that God revealed His glory through the lens of His grace. In fact, grace is not merely the doorway into salvation—it is the atmosphere of this divine relationship. God deals with us only through grace; we receive from Him only by grace.

For this reason, grace must shape a leader's entire worldview. A grace-formed leader relates to God with humility, to others with mercy, to themselves with honesty, and to the world with hope. Without this foundation, leadership easily becomes performance-driven, pride-centred, and justice-skewed. Jonah's story is a prophetic confrontation of such distortions, challenging us to see how offensive grace can be—especially to those who think they've earned it.

Jonah as a Leadership Model

The leadership journey of Jonah begins with a divine interruption:

"*Now the word of the Lord came to Jonah the son of Amittai, saying, 'Arise, go to Nineveh, that great city, and call out against it, for their evil has come up before me.' But Jonah rose to flee to Tarshish from the presence of the Lord...*" (Jonah 1:1–3).

Jonah is not an unfamiliar figure—he is a prophet who had previously prophesied national prosperity during the reign of Jeroboam II (2 Kings 14:23–28). His name, "Jonah," means dove, a symbol used in Hosea 7:11 to represent a senseless and easily deceived Israel. In this way, Jonah becomes a prophetic symbol of senseless leadership—especially in two key areas: (1) how he receives God's grace, and (2) how he resents God's grace extended to others.

Yet, even in his failure, Jonah's full identity reveals hope. His father's name, Amittai, means "truth" or "faithfulness." Jonah, the "son of faithfulness," reminds us that even flawed leaders are still within the reach of God's covenant faithfulness. Grace does not abandon us in our immaturity—it confronts us, shapes us, and sends us again.

In Jonah 1:2, God commands him to arise and preach to Nineveh—a city within the cruel and violent Assyrian empire. Though Nineveh would later conquer Israel, God desires to extend grace to this very enemy. Jonah, however, runs. The disobedient prophet becomes a mirror to every leader tempted to weaponise God's grace rather than channel it. Why did Jonah flee? The text and context expose three internal attitudes that distorted his leadership and obstructed grace:

<u>Three Leadership Barriers to Grace:</u>

1. Monopoly on Grace – Ethnocentrism in Leadership

Jonah resisted the idea that God's grace could extend beyond Israel. His ethnocentric theology imagined God as the exclusive property of His own people. But Psalm 24:1 reminds us, "The earth is the Lord's and the fullness thereof." The grace of God is not a tribal privilege; it is a global mission.

Modern leaders are susceptible to the same narrow mindset—favouring insiders while resisting grace for those who are culturally, socially, or morally "other." Whether due to race, class, sexuality, denomination or political affiliation, when prejudice filters our theology, we become guardians of boundaries instead of channels of blessing. Jesus, by contrast, was moved by need, not worthiness (see Matthew 9). Grace-filled leaders must do the same.

2. Personal Views of Justice – When Prophets Prefer Judgement

Jonah fled not just because of fear—but because of resentment. In Jonah 4:2, he admits that he ran because he knew God would forgive Nineveh. He wanted justice, not mercy. He wanted the enemy punished, not pardoned. His personal views on justice conflicted with God's heart for restoration.

Leaders today often face the same tension. Biblical justice includes consequences, but it also leaves room for redemption. Jonah misjudged both the moment and the method of God's justice. Nineveh would one day be destroyed, but not yet. Mature, grace-shaped leaders discern God's timing. They do not weaponise prophecy to satisfy bitterness. They intercede even for the undeserving—because God's mercy often comes before His judgement.

2. Egocentric Leadership – Rewriting God's Mission

Jonah didn't just reject the mission—he rejected the God who gave it. He ran from the presence of the Lord, replacing obedience with self-interest. His leadership failure wasn't theological—it was personal. He didn't like the assignment. He didn't like the audience. So, he walked away. This is perhaps the most dangerous posture in leadership: when the leader's ego reinterprets the message of God. We become selective with obedience, submitting only to assignments that serve our reputation, our comfort, or our ideology. But true spiritual authority requires surrender. God may call you to deliver grace to the very people who wounded you. Will you obey—or will you run so you can watch them burn?

Jonah reminds us that grace is not just something we receive—it is something we must steward. Leadership shaped by grace refuses to hoard God's mercy, resists the temptation to define justice by personal pain, and rejects the urge to centre self in God's mission.

Throw Him Off the Ship: Confronting Resistance to Grace

Jonah 1:7–16 offers one of the most dramatic and instructive moments in the prophet's journey—a moment that exposes how resistance to grace doesn't remain private. It spreads. It affects communities. It creates storms. "Then they said to one another, 'Come, let us cast lots, that we may know on whose account this evil has come upon us.' So they cast lots, and the lot fell on Jonah..." (Jonah 1:7). When Jonah ran from God, he boarded a ship headed to Tarshish. But the ship wasn't just a mode of transport—it became a theatre of consequence. God's response? He hurled a great wind on the sea. The Hebrew verb used here, "tul" (to hurl), is forceful. God was not passive; He was actively disrupting Jonah's comfort to redirect his calling.

This passage vividly illustrates a key leadership truth: grace resists being weaponised or withheld. Jonah's disobedience put others at risk. The sailors—innocent and reverent—were caught in the crossfire of a prophet's rebellion. Likewise, when leaders reject the assignments of grace, it creates relational, organisational, and spiritual turbulence for those around them.

The narrative makes it clear: the storm wasn't random. God used creation itself—wind, waves, later a fish, then a worm, and a plant—to discipline, redirect, and teach. This is a God who will disrupt our direction in order to preserve our destiny. The storm was not the enemy; it was mercy in motion. Jonah's rebellion endangered others. So often, our personal disobedience isn't just personal. It can destabilise ministries, business, governments, families, teams, and communities. Like Jonah on the ship, we may think our resistance is a private matter, but others begin to feel the swell of the storm we invited. "So, they picked up Jonah and hurled him into the sea, and the sea ceased from its raging." (Jonah 1:15). Sometimes, the only way to restore peace is to confront what's causing the storm. The sailors had to do the hard thing: throw Jonah overboard. This wasn't an act of cruelty—it was an act of surrender to God's greater plan.

Leadership Reflection: What Happens When Grace is Resisted?

Jonah's story is not just about personal rebellion; it's about how one person's response to grace can affect an entire ecosystem. When a leader resists the call of grace, the consequences ripple outward—impacting families, friendships, teams, churches, and even organisations. Grace is never private; it's deeply communal.

- Toxic Patterns or Attitudes

Are pride, fear, bitterness, or control quietly steering your decisions? These internal attitudes may seem manageable, but they create spiritual turbulence around you. Jonah's refusal to surrender led to a storm that endangered everyone on his ship. In leadership—whether in ministry, marriage, or the marketplace—what you carry affects those connected to you. If grace isn't shaping your character, chaos may begin shaping your context.

- Unaligned Relationships

Who are you journeying with, and are they aligned with God's purpose for your life? Jonah wasn't the worst man on the ship, but he was the wrong one. The sailors weren't cursed because of their character—they were caught in a storm because of their company. In leadership, not every partner, employee, or friend belongs in every season. Your openness—or resistance—to grace will determine who thrives around you.

- Self-Sabotage or False Identity

Sometimes, you may be the one creating disruption—not out of evil, but out of unresolved identity or spiritual disobedience. Jonah ran not entirely because he was rebellious, but because he didn't agree with God's mercy. When leaders misalign with grace, they often self-sabotage: second-guessing their calling, avoiding confrontation, or hiding behind titles. Jonah had to be thrown into the deep—not to drown, but to surrender. The sea was his turning point, not his tomb.

Grace in the Throwing

What looks like rejection may be God's redirection. The moment Jonah hit the water, the storm ceased—for everyone. And the fish that swallowed him wasn't wrath, but rescue. It was a womb, not a weapon—a place where grace could finally do its deep work. In your life, God may allow certain "throwings" to happen; endings, disruptions, and even separations. These aren't to punish you, but to purify your path. Grace will sometimes throw your leadership into the deep—not to destroy your influence, but to disinfect your motives.

A Word to Leaders: Your Attitude Toward Grace Sets the Atmosphere

Whether you're leading a church, managing a team, raising a family, or stewarding a vision—your relationship with grace sets the tone. Are you clinging to control, nursing offence, or withholding mercy from others? Those decisions don't just affect you—they affect the climate around you.

- In business, a grace-shaped leader fosters creativity, safety, and growth. A prideful leader breeds fear and instability.
- In friendships, grace allows for restoration and truth; resistance creates distance.
- In family, grace softens hearts and invites healing. Without it, relationships fracture under the weight of unspoken expectations.

Let Jonah Be a Mirror

Ask yourself:

- Is my resistance to grace causing others around me to weather storms they didn't start?
- Is my leadership shaping an environment of restoration—or one of unrest?

Remember: God's grace will confront what we tolerate. It will stir up storms, disrupt toxic calm, and challenge your comfort—not to harm you, but to restore His redemptive purpose in your life and through your leadership. Don't run from grace. Embrace it. It's not just about you—it's about everyone in your boat.

Jonah's Response to God's Grace: Resurrected to Be an Instrument of Grace

In Jonah 1:17, we read: "*And the Lord appointed a great fish to swallow up Jonah. And Jonah was in the belly of the fish three days and three nights.*" The word "appointed" is the first of four references to God's sovereign orchestration in the book—alongside the wind, the worm, and the plant. Jonah may have thought his rebellion took him outside God's reach, but even his disobedience couldn't outrun divine sovereignty. Likewise, we often act as if our poor choices disconnect us from God's plan, but God's grace works even in our lowest moments.

In Jonah 2:1, it says: "Then Jonah prayed to the Lord his God from the belly of the fish." This prayer wasn't immediate. Jonah didn't cry out from the deck of the ship or the surface of the sea. He had sunk. Verses 2–5 describe him at the very bottom of the ocean, seaweed wrapped around his head, fading into unconsciousness. The fish did not intercept him mid-air—it rescued him at the brink of death. Jonah had drowned. The belly of the fish wasn't his punishment; it was his resurrection chamber. Jonah 2:6 declares: "You brought up my life from the pit, O Lord my God." Jonah's literal resurrection is a profound act of grace. It was not earned, deserved, or even requested until the very last moment. But it is precisely this resurrection that transforms Jonah's trajectory. Grace gave him a second chance—not simply to live, but to live with purpose.

Jesus would later refer to Jonah as a prophetic sign: "Just as Jonah was three days and three nights in the belly of the great fish, so will the Son of Man be… in the heart of the earth" (Matthew 12:40). Jonah's temporary resurrection prefigured Christ's ultimate resurrection—where the grace of God burst forth once and for all. Christ's resurrection is the true foundation of grace for all believers. It is not just a spiritual benefit—it is the beginning of our transformation.

Jonah's resurrection reoriented him toward his mission. In the same way, those who have been raised with Christ through grace are called to live differently. Grace doesn't simply restore us—it reassigns us. When we have truly received resurrection grace, we can no longer hoard it or distort it. We become instruments of grace, not just recipients. Jonah's response to grace was repentance—a turning back to his God-given mission of proclaiming mercy to Nineveh. Likewise, for New Testament believers, the right response to Christ's resurrection—the ultimate act of grace—is repentance and faith. Grace doesn't just rescue us; it repositions us to participate in God's redemptive mission to the world. Jonah's journey reminds us: if grace has brought us back from death, then our lives no longer belong to us. The resurrected are on assignment. The mercy that raised us is the same mercy we must now extend—freely, humbly, and without discrimination. Grace received must become grace reflected.

The Compassion Triangle: A Framework for Grace-Filled Leadership

One of the most pivotal sessions I had with my therapist, Adrian, was when he introduced me to the Compassion Triangle—a concept that reframed my entire understanding of grace and leadership. The triangle includes three essential connections: God, self, and others. Adrian explained that compassion is the deep awareness of the suffering of another, accompanied by a strong desire to alleviate that suffering.

Earlier in the introduction, I mentioned that true Christian leadership must be rooted in soteriology—our understanding of salvation through Christ. This framework offers a practical and transformative lens through which to live that out. It helps leaders anchor their ministry in the finished work of Christ while actively engaging in God's redemptive mission. From a Christian standpoint, compassion flows from God to us, and then through us to others. Grace, therefore, is not only a gift we receive, but a life we embody and extend. The Compassion Triangle has radically shaped how I perceive the grace of God—not just as a theological truth, but as a daily calling. It provides a powerful framework for Christian leaders who desire to lead from a place of spiritual alignment, emotional health, and authentic love.

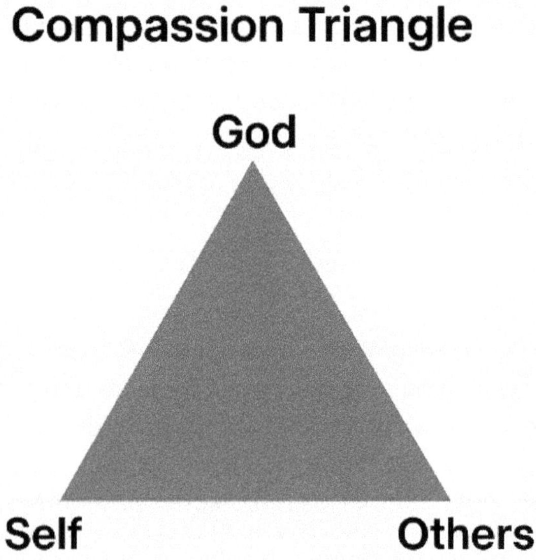

1. God's Compassion – The Source of Grace

God is the origin of all true compassion. He took the first step toward humanity by sending Jesus to suffer on our behalf, alleviating our greatest burden—sin and separation from Him. We don't earn this grace; we receive it by faith because God is compassionate by nature.

We draw from this divine compassion (grace) through:

- Prayer and fasting
- Studying the Word
- Community
- Obedience to God's voice

This connection grounds us. It is our wellspring of identity, peace, and power. Without first receiving God's compassion, we have nothing true or lasting to give.

2. Self-Compassion – Grace Applied Inward

Many people, especially leaders, struggle with harsh self-criticism. What we often overlook is that this inner judgement doesn't just affect our thoughts—it impacts our biology. It activates stress responses and diminishes the body's ability to soothe or regulate itself.

Learning self-compassion means:

- Speaking to ourselves with grace
- Treating ourselves with dignity
- Holding ourselves accountable without shame

This doesn't excuse sin or stagnation—it invites transformation through gentleness and truth. Self-compassion enables us to spiritually and emotionally regulate, so we can lead from a place of rest, not reaction.

It also empowers us to be assertive and set healthy boundaries. When we truly have compassion for ourselves, we recognise our value and stop tolerating what violates our peace, purpose, or integrity. Self-compassion gives us the strength to say “no” when necessary—not out of selfishness, but from a deep sense of God-given worth. We no longer see boundaries as barriers to love, but as expressions of it.

3. Compassion for Others – Grace Poured Out

Only when we've received compassion from God and extended it inward can we truly recognise the suffering of others and respond effectively.

Compassion for others means:

- Seeing beyond behaviour to pain
- Offering help rather than judgement
- Being present, not just performative

True compassion doesn’t mean rescuing—it means reflecting God's heart for redemption. It’s how we become channels of His grace to the world around us.

The Balance: When Compassion Is Misaligned

Adrian also warned of the dangers when the triangle becomes imbalanced. These three misalignments offer a sober reminder:

1. God + Others – Self = Self-Abandonment

When you serve others while neglecting your own soul, you lose yourself in the process.

2. God + Self – Others = Selfishness

When you focus only on personal spirituality and self-growth without compassion for others, you become insulated and ineffective.

3. Self + Others – God = Idolatry

When you care for yourself and others but disconnect from God as your source, you make people or even your own potential the centre of your life.

Final Thought

The compassion triangle invites us to live in balance—receiving deeply, living wisely, and loving freely. As Christian leaders, our ability to embody grace depends on this alignment. Compassion is not a personality trait—it is a spiritual discipline, a reflection of God's very heart. Let this be your framework: From God, through grace, to yourself, and then to others.

Jonah's Response to God's Grace Toward Others: Offended by Mercy

Jonah 4:1–2 states:

"*But it displeased Jonah exceedingly, and he was angry. And he prayed to the Lord and said, 'O Lord, is not this what I said when I was yet in my country? That is why I made haste to flee to Tarshish; for I knew that you are a gracious God and merciful, slow to anger and abounding in steadfast love, and relenting from disaster.*'"

After personally experiencing God's grace in being preserved from death and recommissioned for ministry,

Jonah was furious when that same grace was extended to Nineveh. Though he accepted divine mercy for himself, he was deeply offended when God offered it to others—particularly to a people he considered undeserving. This presents an important lesson for leaders and believers alike: the repentance and restoration of someone else can expose hidden tensions within our own hearts. It becomes a real test of our understanding of grace and maturity in faith.

Grace Offends When We Feel Others Don't Deserve It

In 2 Kings 14:23–25, Jonah previously served as a prophet to King Jeroboam II—a king who "did evil in the sight of the Lord." Ironically, the message God gave Jonah for Jeroboam was one of restoration and prosperity, not judgement. Yet, Jeroboam did not repent. This shaped Jonah's theology: mercy doesn't change wicked people—judgement does. So, when God sent him to Nineveh—a city infamous for its cruelty—it triggered deep offence. How could God show compassion to a people Jonah thought should suffer? This mindset is not unique to Jonah. Consider the parable of the Prodigal Son (Luke 15). The older brother, who had remained dutiful, was angry at the father's extravagant compassion for the rebellious son. Grace toward others unearthed resentment, entitlement, and a misunderstanding of the father's heart. The danger is real: we can be in the house of God and still not understand His heart. Take David and Lucy, for example. They were married for ten years and would often physically fight and curse at each other—sometimes in front of their three children. At the time, they were clearly not in a position to lead anyone. Yet their pastor chose to extend grace, walking with them through their journey. That grace became the foundation for rebuilding their confidence and character.

Then came their test: a younger couple joined their church with a background strikingly like their own. Instead of showing compassion, David and Lucy became irritated, frequently criticising the couple's attitudes and behaviour. Their frustration boiled over—until their pastor gently reminded them, "*This couple is still doing better than you were when you first got married.*" It's a sobering truth: Christians, who are called to be known by their love, are too often known for being judgmental, self-righteous and hypercritical. I've seen this firsthand. Some of the very people I've supported through the most chaotic seasons of their lives have later turned around and acted with harshness and superiority at the first sign of weakness in others. Lord, have mercy on us! That's why humility is vital when approaching the repentance and restoration of others. Galatians 6:1 reminds us to restore others gently, keeping watch over ourselves, lest we too fall into temptation. What kind of temptations might we face? Like David in 2 Samuel 12:1–15, we may find ourselves quick to judge others while remaining blind to our own faults. If left unchecked, this mindset can solidify into the kind of self-righteousness that marked the Pharisees—who were so enraged by Jesus' demonstration of grace that they conspired to kill Him (John 11:45–53).

When Betrayal Tests Your Understanding of Grace

Daniel had joined my ministry and became like family. I invested in him—mentoring with patience, covering weaknesses, and making room for his growth. But over time, I became aware of words spoken behind my back that were damaging and untrue. The discovery stung deeply. I found myself replaying memories, questioning motives, and feeling the sting of betrayal. In my heart, I wanted justice—not in the biblical sense, but in the "I want God to punish him" sense. Have you ever wanted to do the honourable thing, but the other person is acting in a way that makes it even more difficult? If yes that I can relate.

It was even harder because there was no real acknowledgement or repentance, and at times it felt as though the story had been turned on me. I wrestled with my thoughts—Scripture pulling me one way, offence and resentment pulling me another. I could feel bitterness rising whenever his name was mentioned or a message come from him. That's when I knew my heart needed attention. In prayer and in honest conversations with my therapist, the Holy Spirit confronted me gently: "You have done worse to Me—and I forgave you." That truth stopped me and exposed what was hidden in my heart. I saw how easy it is to slip into self-righteousness, forgetting the mercy God has shown me. As leaders, we are called to a higher standard—not to seek revenge or be petty. Forgiveness is not pretending nothing happened— it means surrendering our right to hold resentment and letting go of the desire to see someone else punished. Through prayer, Scripture, and wise counsel, I chose grace and silence over retaliation. In time, God brought the truth to light, dismantling the lies. And as always, He was faithful to vindicate me without my interference.

It's important to note that Scripture does not forbid judgement altogether. Christians are called to exercise discernment (1 Corinthians 5:12; 6:5), especially in matters of leadership and doctrine. But we are warned against judging from a place of arrogance, hypocrisy, or gracelessness. Jonah had passion for God, but he lacked God's perspective. His zeal blinded him to the heart of the One he served. He wanted fire—God offered forgiveness. Jesus warned of this same offence in Matthew 11:6: "Blessed is the one who is not offended by Me."

Leaders and believers must regularly ask:

- Am I offended by how gracious God is to others?
- Does my theology of grace only work when I'm the one receiving it?

Jonah was fervent in his dedication to the Lord. He didn't want Nineveh—a wicked city—to escape punishment. But in his zeal, he failed to grasp the fullness of God's grace and compassion. Likewise, we must ensure that our passion for truth does not make us blind to God's mercy. As Jesus said, "Blessed is the one who is not offended by Me" (Matthew 11:6). Grace offends when we think others don't deserve it. But that's the very definition of grace—undeserved favour. As leaders and followers of Christ, may we carry truth with humility, and conviction with compassion. May we seek His wisdom, that we may not just proclaim His name—but reflect His heart. And may God give us the grace to respond rightly—both to His mercy toward us and His mercy toward others.

Chapter 7 Reflections: Leading by Grace: When Mercy Offends the Religious

Memory Verse

"Each of you should use whatever gift you have received to serve others, as faithful stewards of God's grace in its various forms."— 1 Peter 4:10

Personal Reflection Questions

1. What specific moments come to mind where God's grace carried me, shaped me, or gave me a second chance?
    - Do I truly view my leadership role as a stewardship of grace—or something I've earned?
2. Do I celebrate grace when it's extended to others—even those I struggle with?
    - Have I ever felt threatened, offended, or overlooked when someone else received mercy or restoration?
    - Do I secretly believe they don't deserve what I was freely given
3. Am I ministering grace—or managing judgement?
    - Is my leadership known for mercy, or for measuring others by performance?
    - Do I lead with a restorative heart or a critical spirit?

4. <u>Have I placed limits on where or to whom God's grace can reach?</u>

- Are there types of people—based on culture, background, behaviour, or belief—who I find hard to extend grace to?
- Have I unknowingly hoarded grace for "insiders" and withheld it from "outsiders"?

5. <u>Is God calling me to something I've resisted because it offends my sense of justice or comfort?</u>

- Like Jonah, have I ever said "no" to God not because I can't obey—but because I don't want to?
- What assignment, person, or place have I been unwilling to minister grace to?

6. <u>Is my leadership bringing peace—or stirring storms?</u>

- Are the people around me growing under my leadership, or walking on eggshells?
- Could internal resistance to grace be creating external chaos?

7. <u>What "storms" in my life may be God's mercy in disguise?</u>

- Has God disrupted my comfort to redirect my calling?
- Am I interpreting divine intervention as rejection, when it may be rescue?

8. <u>How can I become a faithful steward of grace in this season?</u>

- What gift or experience of grace have I received that I need to pass on?
- Who around me needs to encounter the grace I've already been given?
- When others receive grace, do I celebrate—or get offended?
- Do I ever feel frustrated when God restores people I think don't deserve it?
- Like Jonah or the older brother in Luke 15, has someone else's restoration stirred resentment in me?

9. <u>What hidden biases or expectations shape my view of who deserves mercy?</u>

- Have I created an internal scale for grace—offering more to those I like or understand?
- Do I believe some people are too far gone for compassion?

10. <u>How do I respond when betrayed by someone I've invested in?</u>

- Have I ever withheld grace in hopes of seeing justice or punishment play out?
- In times of deep personal hurt, do I surrender the offence—or rehearse it?

11. <u>Am I more passionate about truth than I am aligned with God's heart?</u>

- Like Jonah, has my zeal ever outpaced my compassion?
- Do I care more about being right than being redemptive?

12. <u>Which point of the Compassion Triangle am I neglecting right now?</u>

- Am I disconnected from God, harsh toward myself, or judgmental toward others?
- Which imbalance (Self-abandonment, Selfishness, or Idolatry) do I most struggle with?

13. <u>How can I better reflect God's heart in leadership?</u>

- What would it look like to lead from grace—not just gifting or grit?
- Who around me needs the kind of grace I once desperately needed?

<u>Closing Prayer</u>

Lord, Thank You for rescuing me—not only from death but from disappointment and distance. Thank You for the resurrection grace that lifts me from the pit and reassigns me with purpose. Forgive me for the times I've withheld compassion from others, judged harshly, or resented the mercy You so freely give. I admit sometimes I get offended by grace. Sometimes I want justice more than I want healing. But You are not like me. Your ways are higher. Teach me to lead from the heart of Christ—full of truth and full of grace. Give me eyes to see pain behind behaviour, strength to forgive when it hurts, and the wisdom to restore gently. I surrender my offence, my bitterness, and my pride. Help me to love as I've been loved, forgive as I've been forgiven, and extend grace as I've received it. Let my leadership reflect not just Your power, but Your mercy. In Jesus' name, Amen.

Chapter 8

Forged in the Fire: Leading Through Conflict

Conflict is inevitable in leadership, but how we engage it reveals our spiritual maturity, our alignment with Kingdom values, and our capacity to steward both our inner life, and God's mission with integrity. This thesis is not just a starting idea—it is the heartbeat of this chapter. Leadership, especially within the Church, is forged in the fire of human relationships. Regardless of your role or context, how you handle conflict will directly affect your spiritual health, the emotional climate of your organisation, and your ability to faithfully steward the influence God has entrusted to you. This is not merely about avoiding drama—it's about preserving the integrity of your leadership and the atmosphere necessary for mission to thrive. Ministry often involves working with people from diverse backgrounds, wounded histories, and complex personalities. Even without malicious intent, tensions and misunderstandings can—and will—arise. Furthermore, not everyone in the Church comes with pure intentions; some bring unresolved pain, pride, or political agendas. Like any family, the family of God is not immune to dysfunction. What sets healthy leaders apart is not the absence of conflict, but their Christlike posture within it.

That's why Adrian, my therapist, introduced me to the Drama Triangle—a framework first developed by Stephen Karpman in the 1960s. It maps out a cycle of unhealthy relational dynamics often found in conflict: the Victim, the Rescuer, and the Persecutor. These roles may shift fluidly between people—or even within the same person—depending on the situation. Though instinctive and common, each role represents a dysfunctional way of handling tension. And when leaders are pulled into this triangle, it doesn't just drain their emotional energy—it distorts their spiritual atmosphere, clouds their discernment, and undermines their ability to lead from a place of peace and purpose.

In leadership, your response to conflict will either mirror the culture of the Kingdom or feed into the chaos of the world. Left unexamined, someone else's dysfunction can quietly become your atmosphere. But when handled with spiritual maturity, inner alignment, and Kingdom values, conflict can become a crucible for growth, deeper trust, and redemptive clarity.

The Drama Triangle

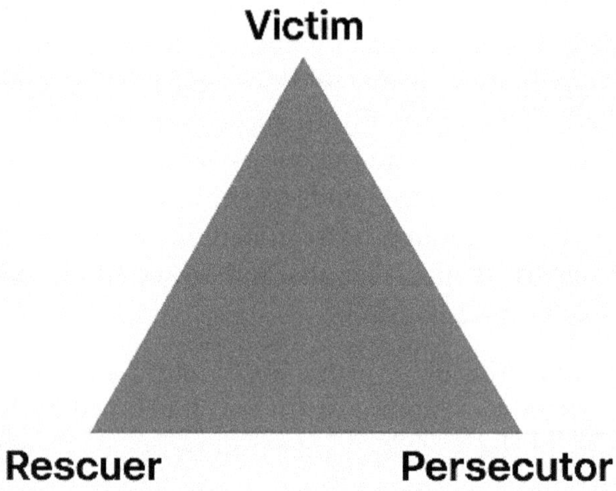

1. <u>The Victim – "Poor Me."</u>

Within the Drama Triangle, the Victim is the one who feels powerless, oppressed, and at the mercy of people, circumstances, or even their own internal struggles. This isn't just a feeling—it becomes an identity. The Victim says, "Life is happening to me, and there's nothing I can do about it." They see themselves as trapped, incapable of changing, and often believe others (the Persecutors) are to blame for their pain. This mindset resists responsibility and places hope in external "Rescuers" to save them—relationally, emotionally, or spiritually. While Victims often stimulate compassion, their posture can become a trap. If they remain fixated on their powerlessness, they forfeit the ability to make meaningful decisions, solve problems, or grow. They may feel sincere in their pain, but without a shift in mindset, they get stuck in cycles of helplessness and disappointment. And in ministry settings, this plays out in particularly challenging ways.

Many people who come into your church or ministry truly are hurting—genuinely seeking refuge, care, and direction. But some, knowingly or unknowingly, adopt a victim posture and begin to expect rescue instead of transformation. They may even weaponise your empathy, subtly manipulating you into carrying responsibilities that aren't yours. Over time, this dynamic creates emotional dependency, where your efforts to help only reinforce their helplessness. In essence, their dysfunction thrives because someone else—often the leader—is absorbing the cost of their stagnation. As I mentioned earlier in this book, leaders often bring their unresolved childhood roles into how they engage conflict. A person can hold a position of spiritual authority—a pulpit, a title, or a platform—and still function like a Victim. They may outwardly lead but inwardly carry wounds, fears, or a martyr complex that causes them to retreat from challenge, avoid confrontation, or blame others for outcomes. They feel overburdened but under-supported, all while unconsciously reenacting the "poor me" narrative. This is why the way we engage conflict matters. As leaders, we must discern when empathy becomes enabling, when helping becomes rescuing, and when someone's Victim posture is not just draining us—but also distorting the spiritual atmosphere we are called to cultivate. If we are to lead with integrity and steward God's mission well, we cannot afford to be pulled into cycles that exhaust us, disempower others, and sabotage the redemptive work God wants to do in their lives.

When the Church Becomes a Restaurant

Over the years in ministry, I've come to see that one of the greatest needs in the Church today is a stronger, healthier ecclesiology—a true understanding of what the Church is and what it means to belong to it. Sadly, many believers in the West approach church not as a family or a mission-centred community, but more like a spiritual restaurant. They arrive with a tailor-made discipleship order:

- For starters, they want to be pampered.
- For the main course, they want affirmation.
- And for dessert, they want their talents celebrated and their ambitions platformed, regardless of faithfulness.

But God forbid you bring correction or speak truth in love—because, for some, conviction has become an allergy! In this consumerist model of church, spiritual growth is traded for self-protection, and genuine accountability is seen as offence. This distorted approach to discipleship sets the stage for roles like the Victim in the

Drama Triangle to flourish unchecked. Let me share a real example that brings this to life.

The Story of John: Potential Undermined by Posture

John was an incredibly gifted Christian—a leader with charisma, spiritual insight, and a heart that initially seemed teachable. But over time, two consistent patterns began to emerge:

- Conflict followed him. His name surfaced regularly when tensions arose.
- There were ongoing complaints about financial integrity—particularly that he borrowed money from people and didn't pay it back.

Despite these red flags, he was extended significant support including training, pastoral care, and even ministry opportunities. But it became increasingly clear: John's priority was John. He longed for visibility, not accountability. When he didn't receive the platform or recognition, he believed he deserved, he left.

Months later, I received a call from his new pastor and his wife. They shared that when they tried to bring loving correction, John became defensive and shifted blame. He told them his former church (my ministry at the time) had "suppressed his gifts" and "never supported him." But before I could respond, they stopped me. "No need," they said. "We've already heard the same story from our team that John is now telling people about his current church!"

It grieved me. John had so much potential—truly. But his Victim mindset was sabotaging his relationships and slowly undermining his calling. He had made his pain and unmet expectations the lens through which he viewed leadership, and in doing so, was deaf to truth and blind to growth.

Leadership Must Call It Out, But With Grace

Stories like John's are not rare. They remind us that spiritual giftedness without inner maturity is dangerous—for the person and the people around them. If leaders are not equipped to name, confront, and pastorally guide people out of the Victim role, we risk enabling emotional immaturity in the name of compassion. And if we ourselves are not careful, we may become Rescuers—pouring out emotionally and spiritually in ways that keep others stuck. When we don't deal with these dynamics head-on, they don't just drain us personally—they can pollute the atmosphere of our ministries. This is why how we handle conflict isn't just a skill issue; it's a spiritual issue. It reveals the state of our hearts, our alignment with Kingdom values, and our capacity to steward both our inner lives and God's mission with integrity.

2. The Rescuer – "Let Me Help You."

Rescuers often show up with good intentions—but not always healthy ones. They intervene on behalf of others, especially Victims, to "save" them from perceived harm or discomfort. On the surface, this looks compassionate. But beneath it, the Rescuer is often motivated by guilt, fear, or a need for validation. Their help becomes a form of self-protection: if I can fix this person, I can feel okay about myself. Rescuers struggle to stand by and "watch people drown." Instead of allowing others to take responsibility for their choices or grow through natural consequences, Rescuers offer short-term fixes that keep people dependent.

Over time, this dynamic not only harms the Victim—it drains the Rescuer. They become fatigued, resentful, and overwhelmed, constantly firefighting other people's chaos while neglecting their own souls. Rescuers often say yes to others but no to themselves—and eventually, no to God's invitation to deeper rest and healing. I know this role all too well—because I lived it.

When Helping Others Becomes Hiding

Before I share this part of my journey, I want to be clear: this is not written as an indirect message to anyone, nor is it about blaming others. My heart in sharing is to testify of God's restoration in my life and to encourage leaders to guard their own wholeness.

After COVID I entered a serious relationship that seemed promising but abruptly ended. Relationships are complex and it takes two, but it felt incredibly painful. Rather than grieving, I distracted myself at times by focusing on ministry and serving others. Not long after that came another deep wound—the unexpected loss of a close friend. The grief from both the breakup and bereavement, combined with the pressures of leading a church through seasons of loss, left me emotionally and spiritually depleted. Instead of giving myself permission to grieve, I continued serving and my pain was buried under the demands of serving others. The needs around me seemed too urgent, and I felt too guilty to withdraw. Instead of resting, I worked harder. I pushed through, ignoring my own emotional, physical, and spiritual depletion. And here's the truth: when you neglect parts of yourself long enough, you start to malfunction. In my case, old struggles & sin I thought were long gone began to resurface. I slipped into patterns I had previously left behind. I was showing up for others while quietly neglecting my own healing—I was playing the role of The Rescuer - trying to rescue others without stopping to acknowledge the fact that I was in need of God's rescue myself.

I began to see that this constant "pouring out" without the attention my soul truly needed had consequences. The cracks began to show—not just in my energy, but in my thinking, my rhythms, and my ability to lead from a healthy place. When certain parts of my story became known years later, the reaction from some wasn't compassion—it was judgement and withdrawal. The hurt was real. I found myself wrestling with the question, "After all I've poured into serving the Body, why would I be treated by some people in this way?" As I brought that pain before God, He gently showed me a deeper truth: "Emmanuel, the hurt isn't only about how you felt you were treated—it's also about how you allowed yourself to change in order to meet the needs of others." In my desire to love and protect, I let go of things back then that I now see as sacred—my boundaries, my rest, my emotional health – all under the banner of 'ministry'. I called it sacrifice, but in reality, it was self-abandonment. And when sacrifice loses its alignment with God, it opens the door to burnout, imbalance, and eventual compromise.

Through restoration and repentance, God began to show me that some of what I had called "sacrifice" was not as aligned with His heart as I once thought. In my desire to serve, I surrendered sacred non-negotiables—my health, my rest, my spiritual rhythms, my boundaries. That wasn't love; it was self-abandonment dressed as ministry. My hurt toward others wasn't only about their actions—it was also about how I had neglected what God entrusted me to steward: myself.

As I repented, the resentment dissolved. I resolved that my service would no longer come at the cost of my own wholeness, nor be driven by guilt or a need for approval. My ministry is unto the Lord alone. I redefined my non-negotiables, set clear boundaries, and embraced rest. With God's comfort and trusted counsel, I rebuilt from the inside out. It feels like a world away from the broken man I once was. I have long since stepped into a new dimension of wholeness—free from resentment, free from relapses, free from unhealthy rescuing, and serving from overflow, not depletion. I am no longer a rescuer.

To every leader reading this: Serving others is a sacred calling, but if you consistently sacrifice your soul, your Sabbath, or your family at the altar of ministry, it may birth bitterness, and you will likely lose yourself —and ultimately make your service impure in God's sight. God sees you, even when others don't. He will reward you. But never forget: your wholeness is not optional. It is essential. Your integrity, peace, and longevity depend on it.

3. Persecutor – "It's all your fault."

The Persecutor plays the role of the accuser. They are often controlling, highly critical, and quick to blame. Like a harsh inner critic or a 'strict parent,' they operate from a belief that they must dominate or "win" the situation, no matter the relational cost. Their version of leadership is rooted in fear, not faith; in control, not compassion.

Persecutors tend to view others—especially Victims—as the problem. They correct harshly but fail to nurture. They set boundaries, but without grace. They are excellent at identifying what's wrong but rarely invested in empowering others to grow through it. They often criticise

Rescuers for being "too soft," without offering meaningful solutions themselves.

But here's the sobering truth: many leaders, particularly under stress, can slip into Persecutor mode—often without realising it. Because this role is performance-driven and perfectionist, it can be masked as excellence or "high standards," when in reality, it's fear-based control. The Persecutor can bully others emotionally, spiritually, or through passive aggression. Their need to manage outcomes makes them resistant to feedback and blind to their own shortcomings.

Like the Victim and the Rescuer, the Persecutor is also deeply preoccupied—but rather than being preoccupied with helping or being helped, they are consumed with assigning blame. Their focus narrows to who is at fault rather than what needs healing or changing. In this fixation, they miss the broader redemptive work God may want to do. A leader acting from this space will eventually damage both people and atmosphere. Their leadership may look competent on the outside, but beneath the surface, they're cultivating fear instead of faith, rigidity instead of restoration, and compliance instead of transformation.

A Heart Check for Leaders

Persecutors don't always look like loud bullies. Sometimes they are sharp with emails, icy with silence, or rigid in team culture. If you find yourself in constant correction mode, irritated at people's weaknesses, or always preparing for conflict rather than restoration—you may be leading from the wrong spirit. The invitation from Jesus is clear: "Blessed are the peacemakers" (Matt. 5:9), not the faultfinders. Kingdom leadership is not about suppressing weakness, but shepherding people through it with truth, grace, and accountability.

Fictitious Examples of the Drama Triangle in Action

Demonstrating how unaddressed conflict patterns in everyday settings can undermine spiritual maturity, team dynamics, and Kingdom impact.

1. Example 1: The Workplace

Conflict erupts not because of the workload—but because of how team members engage from roles of blame, rescue, or helplessness.

Kerry (Persecutor):

“Alex, the report is due by 12 p.m. I’ve told you this already—why hasn’t it been sent?” (Blaming tone, demanding accountability without support.)

Alex (Victim):

“I’m sorry... I was confused about what you wanted, and I’ve just been drowning in other tasks.” (Helplessness, avoidance of responsibility.)

Kerry (Persecutor):

“We sent the template last week. If you didn’t understand it, why didn’t you take the initiative and ask?” (Criticism, control without empathy.)

Alex (Victim):

"I just couldn't keep up. I've been doing everything alone." (Powerlessness, self-justification.)

Kerry (Persecutor):

"It's 10 a.m.—pull something together now. This isn't negotiable." (Commanding, pressure without collaboration.)

Kathy (Rescuer):

"Kerry, I can get the info you need from our programme team—what exactly do you need?" (Jumping in to fix, assuming responsibility for others.)

Kerry (Rescuer shift):

"I just need the standard report update. Thanks, Kathy." (Temporarily shifting into helper mode, still not addressing deeper issues.)

Kate (Persecutor):

"We've done three of these already this week. Can't you reuse one instead of dumping more on us?" (Passive-aggressive blame.)

Kerry (Victim):

"You think I have time? I'm holding this whole thing together by myself." (Overburdened, seeking pity or validation.)

Alex (Persecutor):

"Honestly, this whole reporting process is ridiculous." (Attacking the system, deflecting from their own responsibility.)

Kate (Rescuer):

"Never mind—I'll do it. Just give me thirty minutes." (Saves the day but reinforces dependency and personal burnout.)

Reflection: In the absence of clear boundaries and mutual responsibility, the office atmosphere becomes reactive. No one is truly solving the issue—only cycling through blame, burnout, and short-term fixes.

2. <u>Example 2: The Church</u>

What starts as a pastoral check-in escalates into a cycle of unmet expectations, blame, and rescuing—all under the guise of spiritual concern.

Pastor (Persecutor):

“Hey, I noticed you’ve missed the last two services. It’s really important you’re consistent in showing up.” (Corrective tone, applying pressure without inquiry.)

Church Member (Victim):

“I’m just overwhelmed. Life is really hard right now.” (Powerlessness, subtle guilt appeal.)

Pastor (Persecutor):

“I hear that, but being present might actually help you cope better.” (Mild coercion masked as concern.)

Church Member (Persecutor shift):

“Honestly, no one here really cares about me. You only notice when I’m missing.” (Blame disguised as vulnerability.)

Pastor (Victim):

“I try my best, but I can’t personally engage every member all the time.” (Overwhelmed, deflecting accountability.)

Church Member (Rescuer):

“You really need an assistant. I’d be happy to help or suggest someone.” (Offering to solve the pastor’s issue, seeking value or place.)

Pastor (Rescuer):

“Do you need a lift to church? I can connect you with someone who drives.” (Quick fix solution, avoids addressing root issues.)

Church Member (Victim):

“Yes please. I’ve been struggling with that, and it’s made it hard to come.” (Returning to helpless posture.)

Reflection: This cycle shows how a leader’s over-functioning and a member’s unhealed wounds can create unnecessary tension. True spiritual leadership steps off the triangle—offering truth with grace, support with boundaries.

3. Example 3: The Family

The home becomes an emotional battlefield when each person acts from reactivity instead of responsibility. Even love can get entangled in rescue.

Dad (Persecutor):

“Your room is a mess, and I told you to clean it two hours ago. Get it done—now.” (Aggression, control without compassion.)

Son (Victim):

"I know... but I'm so tired from school and I haven't even eaten yet." (Passive, overwhelmed, seeking pity.)

Dad (Persecutor):

"I don't want excuses. You're not the only one with responsibilities." (Dismissive, unsympathetic enforcement of rules.)

Mum (Persecutor toward Dad):

"What's going on in here? You could have asked me—I've been home all day!" (Blaming Dad instead of resolving conflict.)

Dad (Victim):

"I've been swamped with work all day and now I'm the bad guy? I'm exhausted too!" (Powerlessness, self-justification.)

Dad (back to Persecutor):

"Clean your room now or you're grounded!" (Control, threats as a solution.)

Mum (Rescuer):

"Come on, sweetheart—I'll help you tidy up." (Solving the problem for him, not with him, avoiding discipline or responsibility.)

Reflection: Without emotional awareness, this family cycles between blame, guilt, and rescue—none of which promote growth. Real maturity means moving beyond reactivity to healthy responsibility and compassion.

Are You a Victim, Rescuer, or Persecutor?

The Drama Triangle is a relational model that describes how people unconsciously fall into three reactive roles during conflict:

- Victim – "Poor me."
- Rescuer – "Let me help you."
- Persecutor – "It's all your fault."

These roles are not fixed. In fact, individuals can shift between them rapidly—even within the same conversation—depending on how the interaction unfolds. This role-switching is what keeps conflict cycles alive and confusing.

Susan: switching between roles

For the sake of teaching, I'll use the name Susan—though the details have been adapted and do not point to any specific individual. Susan was a confident and outspoken member of a church community. She could address issues directly, which is often a strength, but in certain moments she struggled to take ownership of her actions. In one situation, when challenged, she took on the Persecutor role—placing blame on leadership in a strong and critical tone. When she noticed her approach wasn't working, she shifted into the Victim role—expressing hurt and disappointment, in the hope of triggering guilt and empathy to achieve her aim. Her tone changed, but her goal remained the same: control through emotional pressure. If you've ever been in a conversation where someone moved quickly from being aggressive to appearing fragile and wounded, you may have experienced that same moment of disorientation. Often, that's a sign you've been drawn into the Drama Triangle—a cycle of shifting roles that keep the conversation trapped in unhealthy dynamics.

In many conflicts, people will unconsciously shift roles to gain influence or regain control. Recognising this pattern is crucial, especially for leaders. When you identify a role shift happening, take a step back. Don't play into the game. Instead, respond from a place of clarity, calm, and conviction. Be mindful of the roles at play. Just because someone sounds vulnerable doesn't mean they aren't trying to dominate the situation—and just because someone is helping doesn't mean they aren't enabling dysfunction.

Breaking the Cycle: From Drama to Empowerment

Recognising the patterns of the Drama Triangle is the first step, but breaking out of it requires intentional transformation—both in how we see ourselves and how we engage others. David Emerald Womeldorff offers a powerful framework in what he calls The Empowerment Triangle (TET). This model reframes the reactive roles of Victim, Rescuer, and Persecutor into life-giving, constructive alternatives:

- The Victim becomes the Creator
- The Rescuer becomes the Coach
- The Persecutor becomes the Challenger

<u>The Empowerment Triangle</u>

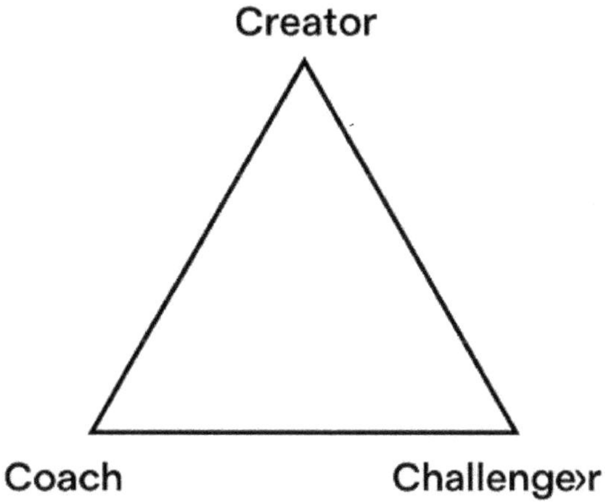

This shift is more than just new labels—it reflects a deeper transformation of mindset and spiritual posture. It moves us from reacting to conflict in fear or ego, to responding with clarity, responsibility, and love. As leaders, this transformation equips us to engage conflict in a way that honours both the truth and the people involved.

1. From Victim → Creator

Instead of being powerless and stuck, the Creator takes ownership of their response and seeks solutions. They don't deny their pain, but they also don't stay defined by it. In fact, they don't waste their pain! Spiritually, this reflects a renewed mind (Romans 12:2), choosing faith over helplessness and action over avoidance.

- Ask: "What is God inviting me to learn or build in this situation?"

2. From Rescuer → Coach

Rather than saving others from discomfort (often to our own detriment), the Coach empowers others by asking questions, offering perspective, and walking alongside them—without doing the work for them. This models Jesus' own way of discipling: truth in love, with boundaries.

- Ask: "How can I support this person without removing their responsibility?"

3. From Persecutor → Challenger

The Challenger brings truth, accountability, and healthy pressure for growth—but with the goal of building up, not tearing down. This role honours the prophetic call to speak truth, but in the spirit of grace and redemptive purpose.

- Ask: "How can I challenge this issue in a way that leads to growth, not shame?"

1. <u>The Workplace – Empowerment Triangle</u>

Context: A report is late. The goal is accountability and partnership, not blame or rescuing.

Kerry (Challenger – Offers growth-oriented accountability):

"Alex, I noticed the report hasn't come through yet. This is important for the portfolio update. Can you help me understand what's in the way so we can move forward?"

(She challenges without shame, creating a space for truth and responsibility.)

Alex (Creator – Takes ownership of his situation):

"Thanks for asking. I realise I missed the deadline, and I've been feeling overwhelmed by conflicting tasks. I could use help thinking through how to prioritise better moving forward."

(Instead of acting helpless, he names the problem and looks for solutions.)

Kerry (Challenger – Sets clear boundaries while encouraging growth):

"I appreciate your honesty. I'd like to challenge you to block out time each week to manage your key deliverables. Let's work out a better workflow together."

Kathy (Coach – Supports without taking over):

"Alex, would it help if I showed you how I organise my report tasks? Maybe we could check in mid-week to make sure things stay on track."

(She doesn't do the work for him—she equips him with tools and accountability.)

Alex (Creator):

"That would really help, thanks. I'd also like to develop a system that works for me long term. I'm ready to make that shift."

Reflection: Instead of Kerry blaming (Persecutor) or Kathy rescuing, the team works together using clear challenge and wise coaching. Alex owns his role as a Creator, stepping out of helplessness and into problem-solving. These dynamics foster personal growth and team health.

2. <u>The Church – Empowerment Triangle</u>

Context: A church member has been missing services. The pastor seeks reconnection, not guilt or control.

Pastor (Challenger – Cares enough to confront with grace):

"Hi! I've missed seeing you lately. I know life can be heavy, but I also believe consistent connection really supports our spiritual growth. How are things going?" (Challenges without judging; invites the member into spiritual ownership.)

Church Member (Creator – Acknowledges their struggle without blame):

"Thanks for reaching out. Honestly, I’ve been struggling with motivation and feeling unseen. I want to grow, but I’m not sure where to begin." (They avoid playing victim, expressing a desire for change.)

Pastor (Coach – Guides toward support without enabling):

"That’s a helpful insight. Would you be open to a quick weekly check-in or joining a small group? You don’t have to figure it out alone."

Church Member (Creator):

"I’d like that. Having someone to walk with me would make a difference. I’ll also commit to being present, even when it’s tough."

Pastor (Challenger – Speaks life into their journey):

"That’s a great next step. I believe God is working in you, and I want to support that journey—not just attendance, but transformation."

Reflection: The pastor doesn’t shame, beg, or ignore—they challenge with care and coach toward action. The church member moves from passive frustration to personal ownership. This is what it looks like to disciple people out of a victim mindset and into spiritual maturity.

3. <u>The Family – Empowerment Triangle</u>

Context: A son hasn't cleaned his room. Instead of blame or rescuing, the parents engage with maturity, clarity, and support—while setting expectations.

Dad (Challenger – Names the issue and sets a clear boundary):

"Son, I asked you to clean your room two hours ago. I understand school can be tiring, but part of growing up is learning to manage both rest and responsibility. I'd like the room cleaned by 7 p.m. tonight. What's your plan for making that happen?" (He combines empathy with a clear deadline and invites his son to take ownership.)

Son (Creator – Acknowledges the struggle and commits to action):

"You're right, Dad. I was wiped out after school and needed a break, but I'll get started after dinner and set a timer so I stay focused. I'll make sure it's done by 7." (He doesn't blame or avoid—he responds with intention.)

Mum (Coach – Offers strategic support, not rescue):

"Would it help to start with just one area—like your desk? Tackling smaller parts can make it feel more doable. I'm happy to talk through a routine if you want help keeping it tidy each week." (She equips him with tools, not shortcuts.)

Son (Creator):

"That actually sounds helpful. I'll start with the desk and keep building from there. I want to handle this on my own."

Dad (Challenger – Affirms effort and reinforces vision):

"That's what I like to hear. Taking ownership is part of becoming a young man. We're here to support your growth, not to nag or rescue you."

Reflection: As someone who has been a professional social worker for several years, I've seen all manner of family dynamics—some deeply dysfunctional, others resilient and redemptive. What I've consistently observed is that healthy families don't avoid conflict—they engage it with clarity, care, and accountability. In this scenario, the father brings clarity, and expectation, not control. The mother offers practical coaching, not over-functioning or enabling. The son responds with self-leadership, not excuse-making. This is how families practically break generational cycles of power struggles, passive aggression, or co-dependency—and instead raise children who are responsible, emotionally secure, and empowered to thrive in the real world.

Why This Matters for Leadership

When leaders operate within the Drama Triangle, we don't just get emotionally drained—we unintentionally distort the spiritual and emotional atmosphere of our teams, families, and churches. However, when we engage conflict from the lens of the Empowerment Triangle—as Creators, Coaches, and Challengers—we model spiritual maturity, align with Kingdom values, and cultivate a healthier culture, both internally and externally. Conflict is inevitable in leadership. But how we engage it will determine whether we perpetuate dysfunction—or walk in divine wisdom. The examples I've shared in this chapter are not meant to be followed rigidly or applied legalistically. Instead, discern the principles behind them and apply them prayerfully to your specific context, because every relational dynamic and leadership situation is different. The goal is not perfection, but spiritual discernment and transformation. I can say from personal experience: I now walk in so much more freedom and joy, simply because I've learned to recognise when someone is trying to pull me into the cycle—and I refuse. I don't fight every fire. I don't absorb dysfunction. I don't enable emotional manipulation. And because of that, I've seen an increase in peace, authority, clarity, and God's presence in my life and leadership. We are in dangerous times where many are tempted to make their trauma their identity, demanding affirmation rather than transformation. May God give you the grace to lead with courage, the discernment to break cycles, and the boldness to walk in truth. It will not only change you, but it will shape the generations to come.

Action Steps: Escaping the Drama Triangle

If your relationships are entangled in blame, burnout, or power struggles, and you're seeing patterns of low performance, long-term conflict, or resentment it may be time to step out of the Drama Triangle. Here are three powerful steps to shift your mindset and move toward freedom and healthier interactions.

1. Build Self-Awareness

Breaking the cycle begins with recognition.

Ask yourself:

- What role am I playing-Victim, Rescuer, or Persecutor?
- How long have I operated in this role?
- Is this serving me or sabotaging me?
- What new role do I want to embrace?
- What specific action can I take today to move forward?

Self-awareness is not self-condemnation. It is the gateway to growth. Whether you're the over-functioning helper, the silent sufferer, or the one enforcing control-recognising your patterns enables you to stop playing roles and start making real choices.

2. Get Help to Make Sustainable Changes

Awareness without action is not enough. True transformation often requires support systems that help you stay the course.

That might look like:

- Support groups where others are navigating similar challenges
- Mentorship or coaching that helps clarify goals, track progress, and build confidence
- Trusted relationships where feedback is welcomed and accountability is embraced

Stepping out of old relational patterns can feel destabilising at first-but with the right people around you, change becomes not only possible, but powerful.

3. Use NVC: Nonviolent Communication

Dr. Marshall Rosenberg's Nonviolent Communication: A Language of Life (2015) offers a framework that allows for truth-telling without blame, and empathy without enabling. NVC supports deeper connection, emotional clarity, and mutual understanding-even in the midst of conflict.

Here's how you can use it practically:

- Step 1: Identify and express your own unmet need.

All emotions are connected to needs-such as safety, respect, autonomy, love, or understanding. Instead of reacting to what someone did, pause and ask:

"What need of mine is this emotion connected to?"

Example: "I felt angry when you interrupted me in the meeting, because I need respect and to have my voice considered."

- Step 2: Identify the need behind the other person's behaviour.

Even if they come across as rude, defensive, or irrational look beyond the tone. They may not be expressing a need, but rather an opinion, judgement, or analysis.

Ask: "What unspoken need might be driving their behaviour?"

Example: Their raised voice could reflect a need for safety or to be heard.

- Step 3: Clarify and verify both sides' needs.

Mutual understanding is key. Once you've named your need and listened for theirs, check in: "I've shared my need for respect, but I wonder if you're feeling a need for safety-is that right?" If they say no, follow with: "Would you be willing to share what you need right now?"

- Step 4: Offer empathy until both needs are understood.

This may require patience. Don't rush the process-create space for clarity and compassion.

- Step 5: Co-create a solution using positive action language.

Once both sides feel heard, then propose strategies that meet both sets of needs.

Frame your solution in terms of what you can do-not just what should stop.

Final Reflection

I've applied these principles, and I can honestly say: they've transformed me. I've become more compassionate, assertive, and grounded. Nonviolent Communication is not about being passive or soft-it's about walking in real power. It enables us to stay connected to others, but also to ourselves, even in moments of tension or disagreement.

So much of leadership is about resisting emotional reactivity and cultivating wise, bold but life-giving responses. We're living in a time where many are tempted to make their trauma their identity, seeking constant affirmation rather than transformation. May God give you the grace, courage, and discernment to lead through the fog-especially when conflict comes.

- Refuse to get pulled into the cycle.
- Stand firm in truth and grace.
- Lead with compassion, boldness and clarity.

Because when you change how you engage conflict, you won't just change conversations-you'll change your culture, your calling, and the generations to come.

Chapter 8 Reflections: Forged in the Fire: Leading Through Conflict

Memory Verse

So that the tested genuineness of your faith—more precious than gold that perishes though it is tested by fire—may be found to result in praise and glory and honour at the revelation of Jesus Christ. – 1 Peter 1:7

Personal Reflection Questions

1. Which role in the Drama Triangle do I most often find myself playing—Victim, Rescuer, or Persecutor?
2. How has this shown up in my leadership, family, or friendships?
3. When I experience conflict, do I typically react emotionally or respond prayerfully?
4. What indicators reveal when I'm slipping into old patterns?
5. What are some 'non-negotiables' I've sacrificed in the name of service or leadership?
6. Have those sacrifices led to freedom or resentment?
7. Have I ever used spiritual language to justify dysfunction in my relationships or avoid healthy boundaries?
8. What truth is the Holy Spirit revealing to me now?
9. How can I become more of a Creator, Coach, or Challenger in my relationships?

10. What is one practical step I can take this week to shift how I respond to tension?

11. Do I know the difference between compassion and co-dependency?

12. How can I show kindness without losing clarity?

13. What trauma, unmet need, or past experience might be influencing how I engage in present conflict?

14. Have I invited God or wise counsel into that space?

15. Who helps me remain accountable to healthy boundaries and Christlike conflict resolution?

16. Am I willing to be challenged in love?

Closing Prayer

Father God, Thank You that You are not a God of confusion or dysfunction—but of peace, wisdom, and clarity. I confess the ways I've been drawn into unhealthy patterns of rescuing, blaming, or withdrawing. Show me where I've exchanged truth for comfort, control for compassion, or sacrifice for performance. Teach me to lead like Jesus: with grace and truth. Make me bold enough to confront with love, wise enough to set boundaries, and humble enough to change. Help me discern when someone is pulling me into a destructive cycle and give me the strength to stand in truth and presence. I choose freedom. I choose maturity. I choose to reflect Your Kingdom, even in the middle of conflict. In Jesus' name, Amen.

Chapter 9

Vulnerability: A Leader's Hidden Strength

Vulnerability is not a liability in leadership—it is a strategic asset when expressed with wisdom and in the right context. When leaders are vulnerable in the right way and with the right people, it fosters authentic connection, builds trust, deepens dependence on God, and inspires others to walk in honesty, courage, and transformation. Vulnerability models a kind of strength that performance alone can never produce. This chapter explores Jesus' model of vulnerability, highlighting how His openness and authenticity were a source of strength rather than weakness. We will examine the powerful benefits of biblical vulnerability in leadership—including fostering deeper connection, authenticity, and dependence on God. Finally, practical guidance will be provided on how to safeguard your vulnerability, ensuring it is shared wisely and protected against exploitation.

Jesus: A Model of Vulnerability that Empowers Others

"*Now Thomas, one of the twelve, called the Twin, was not with them when Jesus came. So the other disciples told him, 'We have seen the Lord.' But he said to them, 'Unless I see in his hands the mark of the nails, and place my finger into the mark of the nails, and place my hand into his side, I will never believe.' Eight days later, his disciples were inside again, and Thomas was with them. Although the doors were locked, Jesus came and stood among them and said, 'Peace be with you.' Then he said to Thomas, 'Put your finger here, and see my hands; and put out your hand, and place it in my side. Do not disbelieve but believe.'*

Thomas answered him, 'My Lord and my God!' Jesus said to him, 'Have you believed because you have seen me? Blessed are those who have not seen and yet have believed.'"— John 20:24-29

All the disciples had seen the risen Jesus except Thomas. When told, Thomas doubted their testimony, suspecting they might have seen a ghost (cf. Matt. 14:26; Mark 6:49). Eight days later, Jesus appears to Thomas and invites him to touch His scars—the very marks of His crucifixion. Thomas responds in awe, declaring Jesus as "My Lord and my God! "This encounter reveals profound insight into Jesus' leadership through vulnerability. Jesus used His human scars—symbols of His suffering and journey—to authenticate His divine identity and process to Thomas. His scars were not marks of weakness but of authentic experience, truth, and triumph.

Scars as Symbols

Scars stand as powerful symbols of the significant moments in our faith journey. They represent the trials we have faced and overcome, inspiring hope and trust in God for others. Just as Jesus' scars testified to His sacrifice and resurrection, our scars are testimonies of God's faithfulness in our lives.

Leadership Implications

From a leadership perspective, Thomas represents those we lead—our teams, congregations, or communities. Thomas was not inspired by a flawless leader; he was moved by a leader who was real, vulnerable, and had scars that spoke of genuine experience. If leaders hide their scars, they risk intimidating rather than inspiring. Presenting an image of perfection can create distance because it's not reflective of the human experience. True leadership invites others in by being authentic about struggles and growth, showing that vulnerability is a pathway to strength and deeper connection.

Braving Vulnerability

I will never forget some of the mentoring sessions I had with Dr. Sharon. There was one in particular when I felt frustrated—because I thought I was being as vulnerable as possible, yet she gently but firmly said, "You're still speaking from your head." At the time, I couldn't fully see it, but looking back, she was right. I didn't realise at the time that I had built protective layers over the years—partly from difficult leadership experiences and partly from challenges in relationships I cared deeply about. When your vulnerability has been mishandled, it's easy to start calculating what you share and with whom. At the time I had unknowingly carried a subtle core belief: "If people really knew certain things about me, they might not value me the same way."

Dr. Sharon shared how she herself had navigated her experiences with her own leaders as well as lessons she learnt with those she led over the years, and that helped me more than I can express. I remember one time after a challenging day, I voiced some things I had rarely said out loud before—reflections on moments in leadership over the years where I had felt stretched, misunderstood, or unsupported. It was uncomfortable to be that open. In fact, I thought 'did I just say that?', but something shifted. That moment allowed Dr. Sharon to see me beyond the role—to see the person. I shared with deep respect, not in dishonour, but in courageous vulnerability. I'm genuinely grateful for the safe space she created because it helped build deeper trust and strengthened our relationship.

Her willingness to be vulnerable, both as a leader and mentor, inspired me deeply. It gave me a template for how to lead and how to be mentored. As God has healed my heart and reshaped my inner beliefs, I've seen the power of wise, intentional vulnerability—not just for personal healing, but for healthy and effective leadership itself. I began to experience richer encounters with God in prayer and even sensed His grace and tangible presence in ordinary conversations. Prophetic insight seemed to flow more freely, and I noticed that a greater authenticity has a way of dismantling invisible walls in others. It was like stepping into a new dimension of hearing and seeing in the Spirit. That's why I write this chapter—because vulnerability, when stewarded with wisdom, shared in safe spaces with the right people, is not weakness. It's one of the most powerful assets a leader can carry.

Real vs. Ideal Leadership: Embracing Authenticity in a Culture of Expectations

In today's culture, leaders face the tension of being held to high standards while also being expected to remain relatable and transparent. Too often, when leaders fail to meet these sometimes-unrealistic expectations, the reaction is quick, harsh, and unforgiving—leaving little space for them to show their humanity. The result? Many leaders feel pressured to present an idealised image, driven by the fear that, "If people see me as I really am, they won't accept me.". Yet, true leadership does not thrive in perfection—it thrives in authenticity. Biblical vulnerability—being real about who we are—is not a weakness, but a profound strength. Sadly, we live in a time where confusion about identity and gender roles has blurred the lines, making strong, godly male leadership less visible and less understood. Vulnerability is often misunderstood as softness or weakness. When I talk about vulnerability, I'm not simply encouraging men to cry more. I'm inviting leaders to connect deeply with themselves and speak genuinely from that place. Real, godly vulnerability is strength under control—courage with humility.

This is why I am so grateful for Dr. Ralph. Over this past year, he has been like a father to me, and his life has been a clear, living model of what godly manhood and leadership look like. In him, I've seen strength anchored in conviction, authenticity without compromise, and vulnerability that invites trust rather than diminishing respect. Our candid conversations have not only challenged and inspired me—they have given me a tangible picture of balance: a man who leads with authority, yet remains approachable, who carries great strength, yet is unafraid to be real. Dr. Ralph's example has reminded me that it is entirely possible—and powerfully impactful—to be a strong man who leads with both truth and tenderness, conviction and compassion. He has shown me that godly male leadership is not about projecting flawlessness, but about leading from a place of wholeness, humility, and courage.

The Benefits of Vulnerability in Leadership

1. Vulnerability Connects People to God's Saving Grace

Paul was a brilliant Pharisee trained under Gamaliel. Yet when sharing the gospel, he didn't rely on intellectual arguments alone. Instead, he vulnerably shared his journey from persecutor of Christians to follower of Christ, showing his flaws and failures. This honest testimony showcased God's mercy and grace, making his message relatable and inspiring.

Just like Jesus revealed His scars to Thomas to confirm His divine nature, Paul displayed his weaknesses to highlight God's strength working through human frailty (1 Timothy 1:15-16, 2 Corinthians 12:9-10). As leaders, sharing our humanity allows others to connect with God's grace, fostering humility and dependence on Him.

Balance is key: share the parts of your story where God's grace is evident. Later in this chapter, we will explore how to protect yourself while being vulnerable.

2. Vulnerability Inspires Others

The church needs testimonies that speak to every human struggle. Without real stories of God's grace at work, how can people believe in His healing and deliverance? When Thomas witnessed Jesus' scars, he responded with awe and faith-"My Lord and my God!" This genuine response shows how vulnerability inspires and encourages others.

3. Vulnerability Provides a Biblical Model

Authentic vulnerability models healthy stewardship of our humanity and God-given identity. Many leaders grew up believing they wouldn't be accepted if they expressed emotions, causing shame and emotional struggles later in ministry. But working through these challenges enables leaders to remain emotionally healthy and deeply connected to God's divine nature.

4. Vulnerability Brings Healing

Confessing our shortcomings brings spiritual and emotional healing (James 5:16). Being vulnerable invites restoration-for ourselves and those we lead.

The Dangers of a Lack of Vulnerability in Leadership

1. Limited Access to Help

Refusing to be vulnerable can harm the leader, their family, and ministry. Vulnerability can be tough, but withholding it often means the strongest leaders receive the least care and support when they need it most.

2. False Leadership Model

When leaders hide their struggles, they unintentionally teach others that leadership requires perfection. This perpetuates a cycle where vulnerability is seen as weakness instead of strength.

3. Restricted Grace

Without vulnerability, we limit God's grace toward ourselves and those we lead. Grace flows most freely when we acknowledge our need and imperfections.

4. Intimidation Instead of Inspiration

A perfect, flawless image can intimidate others, making them feel disconnected and unable to relate. This stifles authentic connection and growth within teams and communities.

The Power of Testimony: A phone call with Luke

I received a call from a friend asking if I would speak to his cousin, Luke. Luke was deeply involved in spirituality and yoga but still held some beliefs about God and deliverance. He was struggling—especially after the conflict he was having with his girlfriend, with whom he had children—and he was looking for answers.

When we first spoke, Luke was formal and reserved, likely because he knew I'm a pastor. But as he shared his struggles and desire for freedom, I sensed it was time to be real. I felt led to share part of my own journey—not every detail, but enough to show that I understood what it's like to wrestle with pain and to seek freedom. I told him about my own battles—how trauma had once driven me into destructive behaviours. I shared how God, in His mercy, met me there, revealing that I was never alone. That truth brought instant freedom. It wasn't my strength that changed me, but God's grace. From that moment, I no longer needed anything external to numb or hide my pain—because Jesus' sacrifice had removed it completely. I explained that salvation is not about selfish gain, but about entering into a genuine relationship with Jesus—turning from sin and trusting Him fully.

Luke was evidently moved by both the gospel and my testimony. Right there, he renounced his past and chose to follow Jesus. Today, he attends his cousin's church and has been baptised. This encounter reminded me of a powerful truth: when we dare to share our story with grace, it becomes the very stage for God's transforming grace to be revealed.

Delilah: A Model of Vulnerability That Disempowers Others

"*How can you say, 'I love you,' when your heart is not with me?*" – Judges 16:15

The story of Samson and Delilah is often told as a cautionary story of betrayal and poor judgement. But at its core, it's a profound lesson about the mismanagement of vulnerability. Samson, a man marked by divine strength, shared the deepest part of himself with the wrong person. It cost him not only his strength, but also his freedom, his sight, and eventually, his life. In an age that champions emotional vulnerability, we must also teach discernment. Vulnerability is powerful, but power without stewardship can be dangerous. Delilah serves as a model of what to watch out for—not just in romantic relationships, but in leadership, friendships, family, and work.

Let's look at the warning signs she presents:

1. Entitlement to Intimacy

Delilah felt entitled to Samson's vulnerability without earning it through character or consistency. She never asked, "Am I trustworthy with this level of access?"

Just because someone is close in proximity—romantically, relationally, or emotionally—does not mean they have earned the right to your secrets.

Lesson: Love does not qualify someone to hold your vulnerability—trustworthiness does.

2. Emotional Manipulation & Guilt

Delilah didn't just ask Samson for his secret she weaponised guilt, using love as leverage. "How can you say you love me if...?" She pressed him daily, breaking him down mentally, emotionally, and spiritually.

Lesson: True love does not manipulate or guilt you into opening up. Pressure disguised as care is still control.

3. No Respect for Privacy

The moment Samson opened up, Delilah ran to the Philistines. She didn't hesitate to expose what was sacred.

Lesson: A safe person protects your dignity, even in your most fragile moments. If someone leaks your secrets, they are not your sanctuary.

4. Weaponising Vulnerability

After shaving his hair, she tormented him. The very thing Samson shared in confidence became the source of his pain.

Lesson: If someone uses your vulnerability against you—whether to hurt you, control you, or shame you—they disqualify themselves from that level of access.

5. Blinding You (Loss of Vision)

Samson lost his physical sight—but often, sharing with the wrong person leads to emotional and spiritual blindness: confusion, distraction, or loss of purpose.

Lesson: If someone's influence causes you to lose clarity, focus, or spiritual direction, it may be time to pull back.

6. Leading to Bondage, Not Freedom

Finally, Samson was bound in chains. Vulnerability with the wrong people can result in emotional, mental, or spiritual captivity.

Lesson: If your openness leads you into shame, fear, or control, that relationship is not a safe space—it's a prison.

Final Thought

We often champion vulnerability as a strength—and it is. But it must be stewarded with wisdom. Delilah reminds us that not everyone who asks for access deserves it. Love alone is not the measure—trust, privacy, protection, and peace are. In every space—relationships, leadership, friendship—discern the difference between safe spaces and snare traps. Vulnerability is sacred. Protect it like a treasure.

When I Spoke to the Wrong Person

Have you ever regretted being vulnerable with the wrong person? I have. Some time ago, I once shared some personal struggles with a leader I respected—only to have my honesty later used in a way that felt deeply hurtful. Critical remarks were made, and indirect comments about me found their way into conversations with other people. When this came to my attention it was devastating.

The betrayal didn't just sting—it triggered old core beliefs I thought I had long outgrown at the time:

- "I am alone."
- "People can't be trusted."

In response, I shut down. I stopped sharing. I pulled away from people and started coping through isolation, believing it was safer to keep everything in. But God didn't leave me there. Through prayer, scripture, and wise counsel, He began to work on my heart. Slowly, I began to challenge those beliefs.

I came to realise that saying "nobody can be trusted" was too extreme, and ultimately untrue. Instead, I learned a more balanced truth: "Some people can be trusted. Others cannot. And wisdom is learning to tell the difference." That shift changed everything. It brought healing. It gave me clarity. And it helped me start managing my vulnerability with discernment, not fear. Now, I don't shut everyone out—but I don't let everyone in either. I listen to character, not just words. I pay attention to patterns, not just promises. And I pray for wisdom to know who is safe for my soul.

Hope — Samson's Hair Grew Back

Reading this may stir up feelings—pain, anger, embarrassment—from times you shared something personal with the wrong person. I get it. I've been there.

But here's the hope: Samson's hair grew back! That small sentence in Scripture carries a powerful message. It reminds us that God's grace can restore what's been lost—even when our trust was misplaced, even when our vulnerability was mismanaged or manipulated.

Despite Samson's choices and Delilah's betrayal, God remembered him. And I want to declare this over you today: God has remembered you too! You may have been hurt. You may feel exposed. You may have lost confidence in people—or even in yourself. But God is a redeemer. He is the God who restores strength, dignity, and hope. What was taken from you doesn't have to be the end of your story. Samson's strength returned. And so will yours.

As you read the rest of this book, you'll begin to see how trust can be repaired, how wisdom can guard your heart, and how God can redeem even the most painful experiences.

You are not beyond restoration. Your story is not over. Your hair will grow back.

Vulnerability Does Not Mean Powerlessness

One essential principle you must hold to protect yourself from emotional exploitation is this:

Vulnerability does not equal powerlessness. Just because you have areas of weakness-or have courageously shared them-does not give others the right to exploit or mistreat you.

Let me give you a few real-life examples of what that exploitation might look like:

- A spouse who feels justified in disrespecting you because they know where you're sensitive.
- A mentee or team member who feels entitled to question your competence or speak rudely to you, using your openness as ammunition.
- Parents who treat you harshly or dismissively now that they see your struggles.
- Friends who gossip about you or mock you behind your back after hearing your story.
- Children who speak down to you or dishonour you because they've seen your humanity.

This is not accountability. This is abuse of access. This is not honesty. This is weaponised familiarity. If your vulnerability causes others to feel hurt, anger, or disappointment, that is valid. Emotions are real and deserve compassion and understanding. But emotional pain does not justify disrespect. They may feel something, but they don't have the right to mistreat you.

Let that truth settle deeply:

- You can be vulnerable and still set boundaries.
- You can be honest and still deserve honour.
- You can be real about your pain without giving others permission to hurt you in return.

Vulnerability is not a weakness to be used- It's a gift to be protected.

Understanding Relationship Categories - Dr. Dharius Daniels' Framework

In his book Relational Intelligence (2020), Dr. Dharius Daniels outlines four key relationship categories that can help you interpret, protect, and steward your relational connections wisely. This framework is especially helpful when trying to discern who is safe for your vulnerability.

1. Friends

While we owe love to everyone, we do not owe everyone access to our inner lives.

True friends are those with whom we share intimate and personal matters. They are relational assets-people who contribute to our personal growth and support us in becoming who God created us to be.

Friendship is built on:

- Consistency
- Commitment
- Love
- Honesty
- Mutual respect
- Nurture and support

These relationships are safe spaces for vulnerability because they are founded on mutual care and trust.

2. Associates

Associates are people we interact with regularly or occasionally, but who do not fall into the categories of friends, advisors, or assignments.

An associate may be someone we get along with socially or professionally, but:

- There has not been enough time, interest, or desire to develop a deeper connection.
- The relationship remains surface-level due to lack of chemistry, differing values, or safety concerns.

It's important not to mistake an associate for a friend just because of the frequency of interaction.

3. Assignments

Assignments are individuals you are called to invest in, such as a mentee, trainee, or someone receiving guidance or support from you. This relationship is more one-sided- you pour into them, not the other way around. This doesn't mean the person is selfish, but rather that the purpose of the relationship is to serve their development, not yours. Trying to be vulnerable with an assignment in the same way you'd be with a friend can lead to imbalance and disappointment.

4. Advisors

Advisors are mentors who provide wisdom, guidance, and support-sometimes for a season, sometimes for a lifetime. They pour into you. In this dynamic, you are the assignment.

It's important to recognise the distinction between advisors and friends, even if the relationship may feel personal. Their primary role is to guide, not walk every step with you.

Why This Matters

Mislabelling relationships can lead to emotional confusion, misplaced vulnerability, and even relational trauma. By learning to discern whether someone is a friend, associate, assignment, or advisor, you can make healthier decisions about:

- What you share
- How much access you give
- What expectations you hold

Wisdom is not just knowing who to love-but knowing how to love them rightly.

Circles of Intimacy, Responsibility, and Impact: A Framework for Christian Leaders

As a Christian leader, understanding your relational boundaries is essential—not just for emotional well-being, but for spiritual sustainability, ministerial effectiveness, and integrity before God. This adapted version of Marilyn Murray's Circles of Intimacy (Earle Jr. & Laaser, 2002, pp. 103-105) helps Christian leaders assess where to invest vulnerability, how to protect sacred spaces, and where your greatest responsibilities lie.

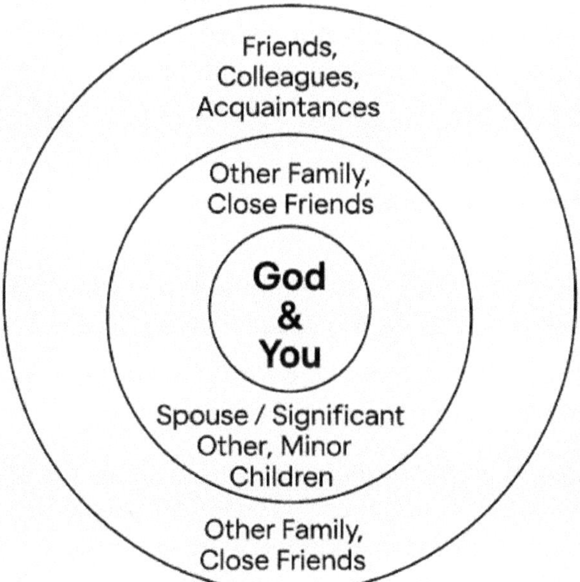

Circle 1: God & You (Sacred Intimacy)

"*Love the Lord your God with all your heart, soul, mind, and strength...*" (Mark 12:30)

- This is your innermost circle. It's where your identity is formed, your soul is anchored, and your leadership is sustained.
- If only you are in this space: you risk narcissism, independence, and emotional isolation.
- If only God is here (and you neglect self-care), you may become a spiritual martyr—self-sacrificing in a way God never asked of you.
- Healthy leadership begins when God and you walk in intimacy, with self-awareness and grace.

Warning: If others (including your ministry, followers, or mentors) enter this space, it can lead to idolatry, co-dependence, and burnout.

Circle 2: Covenant Relationships (Core Family)

"*...The two shall become one flesh... what God has joined together, let no one separate.*" (Mark 10:8-9)

- This circle includes:
  - Your spouse or covenant partner
  - Minor children (living at home)
- This is the space of mutual vulnerability, emotional nourishment, and spiritual unity.

- Challenges and injuries arise when:
    - There is an imbalance in how people include each other in their circle e.g. they are in your circle 2 but you are in their circle 3.
    - You place others (e.g., spiritual sons/daughters, mentors) at the same level as your spouse or children.
    - You neglect this circle for ministry.

Note: Ministry should never replace or compete with this circle. To win the world but lose your family is not success—it's misalignment.

Circle 3: Trusted Friends, Mentors, and Spiritual Family

"*A friend loves at all times, and a brother is born for adversity.*" (Proverbs 17:17)

- These are people you trust with your failures, dreams, and process. They're the ones who pray for you, tell you the truth, and cover you in love.
- Sadly, many leaders have few in this circle. Many are relationally surrounded but emotionally alone.
- You may have:
    - Pastoral peers
    - Spiritual fathers/mothers
    - Counsellors or coaches
    - Long-time friends with shared history and values

Wisdom Tip: Every leader needs at least 1–2 people here who aren't impressed by your platform but care for your soul.

Circle 4: Community, Congregation, and Colleagues

"Be shepherds of God's flock that is under your care, watching over them..." (1 Peter 5:2)

- These include:
    - Church members or ministry teams
    - Extended family
    - Co-labourers in the Kingdom
    - Spiritual mentees, staff, and networks
- While important, these relationships are often assignment-based, not intimacy-based.
- Leaders must avoid oversharing here—emotional dumping or seeking validation.
- You are responsible to serve, lead, and equip this circle, but boundaries are vital.

Guardrail: When leaders seek emotional support from those they're leading, lines blur and trust breaks.

How to Use These Circles as a Leader

- Map your relationships. Who's in each circle?
- Evaluate impact. Who has disproportionate influence over your emotions or decisions?
- Adjust boundaries. Is someone in a closer circle than they should be? Or too far out?
- Review regularly. Seasons change. So do relationships. Review your circles every few months in prayer.
- See Appendix 2 at the back of this book for more guidance.

Final Thoughts for Leaders:

- Responsibility increases as you move outward.
- Intimacy decreases as you move outward.
- Your calling does not excuse emotional recklessness or poor boundaries.
- Jesus had circles: the crowds, the 70, the 12, the 3, and the Father. You must too.

Conclusion

Biblical vulnerability is not weakness—it is a powerful tool when managed with wisdom.

In today's culture, vulnerability is often encouraged, but rarely are we taught how to be vulnerable wisely, with the right people in the right settings. Mismanaged vulnerability—especially in leadership—can lead to disillusionment, mistrust, manipulation, and even deep emotional or spiritual harm.

This chapter was written to help you:

- Discern the difference between safe and unsafe spaces for sharing.
- See the power in being authentic
- Reorganise your relational circles with clarity and intention.
- Heal from the wounds of misplaced trust or spiritual betrayal.

When leaders share their humanity with discernment, they become channels of God's grace to others. Jesus Himself modelled this—He wept, shared His scars, He grew weary, He was tempted—yet He chose His moments and His inner circle with purpose. We are called to do the same. By acknowledging our weakness, we don’t diminish our strength—we access God's supernatural grace. This grace not only sustains us but empowers others to believe that healing and redemption are possible. Vulnerability, when stewarded well, becomes a testimony, a ministry, and a mirror that reflects God's glory. It cultivates humility, keeps us dependent on Him, and reminds us that all honour, all strength, and all victory come from the Lord.

Chapter 9 Reflections: Vulnerability: A Leader's Hidden Strength

Memory Verse

"But he said to me, 'My grace is sufficient for you, for my power is made perfect in weakness.' Therefore, I will boast all the more gladly of my weaknesses, so that the power of Christ may rest upon me." — 2 Corinthians 12:9

Personal Reflection Questions

1. In what areas of my life have I been vulnerable lately? How have I stewarded that vulnerability?
2. Who are the safe people in my life that I can share my struggles and fears with? How have they proven trustworthy?
3. Are there any relationships where I feel my vulnerability has been exploited? How can I set healthier boundaries with those people?
4. How do I personally define vulnerability in the context of my faith and leadership?
5. What negative beliefs or wounds about trust and vulnerability do I need to bring before God for healing?
6. How can I practice humility by acknowledging my weaknesses while still walking in God's strength?
7. What is one small step I can take this week to build or repair trust in a key relationship?

8. <u>How can I use my own story of vulnerability and restoration to encourage and inspire others?</u>

<u>Closing Prayer</u>

Lord, thank You for Your grace that meets me in my weakness. Help me to be wise in how I share my heart and whom I trust. Teach me to walk in humility and courage, knowing that Your strength is made perfect when I am weak. Restore broken relationships and heal the wounds caused by misplaced trust. May my vulnerability be a testimony of Your faithfulness and power. In Jesus' name, Amen.

Chapter 10

The Wounds of Betrayal: Leading Through Pain

Betrayal is a painful but inevitable and refining reality in leadership; how we respond to it shapes our legacy and reveals the heart of Christ within us. Every leader will face betrayal. Whether from a trusted friend, a mentee, a colleague, or even a family member, betrayal pierces deeply because it often comes from those closest to us—those we let into our inner circle. It is not just the act itself that wounds, but the breaking of trust, the misuse of access, and the distortion of love. Even Jesus was not exempt. In this chapter, we will reflect on two betrayals in Jesus' final days: Peter's denial and Judas' betrayal. Both men walked closely with Jesus. Both failed Him. But their stories—and Jesus' responses—could not be more different.

By examining these accounts, we will explore:

- How to process betrayal without becoming bitter.
- How to discern which relationships are worth restoring—and which ones are not.
- How to repair trust in those relationships that are salvageable.

And most importantly, how to reflect the heart of Christ even in our deepest wounds.

Leadership demands wisdom in dealing with broken trust. But more than wisdom, it demands a heart that beats with grace, truth, and clarity. This chapter is for the betrayed—and for the leader who wants to walk the Jesus way even when wronged.

What Is Betrayal?

Betrayal is the deliberate violation of trust. It comes from the Middle English word 'bitrayen', meaning to mislead or deceive. At its core, betrayal involves intentionally acting in a way that harms or exposes someone who has entrusted you with access, affection, or information. Whether it's revealing a secret, acting disloyally, or aligning with an adversary, betrayal cuts deeply because it always involves proximity. You can't be betrayed by a stranger. Only those closest to you-friends, family, partners, or followers etc-can inflict this particular kind of pain.

Examples of betrayal in everyday life include:

- A friend stealing your business idea and running with it behind your back
- A colleague sharing private struggles you entrusted them with.
- A team member partnering with someone who is actively undermining your vision.
- A leader using their position or influence for personal benefit at the expense of others.

In leadership, betrayal is not just painful-it's personal. And how we respond to it can either shape us into Christlike leaders or harden us into defensive ones.

Biblical Examples of Betrayal

The Bible does not shy away from the reality of betrayal. Some of Scripture's most pivotal moments are marked by this painful experience. Here are three key examples:

1. Joseph and His Brothers (Genesis 37:12-28)

Joseph's brothers, driven by envy over their father's favouritism, conspired to kill him. Instead, they sold him into slavery and lied to their father about his fate. This betrayal began Joseph's long road of injustice-but it ultimately positioned him for purpose. His story is a masterclass in forgiveness, faith, and divine providence. It reminds us that betrayal may detour us, but it doesn't destroy God's destiny for us.

2. David, Absalom, and Ahithophel (2 Samuel 15-17)

King David experienced betrayal both in family and in leadership. His own son, Absalom, staged a coup, and David's trusted advisor, Ahithophel, defected to support the rebellion. This double betrayal-familial and political-illustrates the emotional weight leaders carry. David's anguish and prayers in the Psalms reflect a heart wounded by betrayal yet still anchored in God.

3. Jesus and Judas Iscariot (Matthew 26:47-50)

Judas' betrayal is the most infamous in Scripture. A disciple turned traitor, Judas handed Jesus over to the authorities for thirty pieces of silver-with a kiss. Despite walking closely with Jesus, witnessing miracles, and sharing meals, Judas' heart was entangled in greed and darkness. His actions precipitated Jesus' crucifixion, yet they also fulfilled prophecy and opened the door to salvation.

Jesus' Leadership Mindset on Relationships

"*But Jesus would not entrust Himself to them, for He knew all people. He did not need any testimony about mankind, for He knew what was in each person.*" - John 2:24-25

Jesus loved people deeply-but He didn't place unrealistic expectations on them.

He understood the nature of humanity. While many believed in Him because of His miracles, Jesus didn't entrust Himself to everyone. He set emotional and relational boundaries, not from paranoia, but from wisdom. Someone once said, "The best of men are men at best." Even the most well-meaning people can disappoint us. As leaders, we must follow Jesus' example by:

- Loving people without idolising them.
- Expecting failure without becoming sarcastic or pessimistic.
- Entrusting our hearts to God above all.

Jesus' mindset protects us from placing our emotional and spiritual stability in the hands of fallible humans. Leaders who ground themselves in God's faithfulness will be less shaken by people's failures.

Jesus' Model: A Leadership Approach to Betrayal

Betrayal is a painful but refining reality in leadership; how we respond to it shapes our legacy and reveals the heart of Christ within us. Both Judas and Peter betrayed Jesus. Both were apostles, personally called by Him, and operated in power and proximity—yet their outcomes could not have been more different. By analysing Jesus' interactions with each, their heart postures, and ultimate destinies, we gain profound insight into how to lead through betrayal, rebuild trust, and discern which relationships can or cannot be restored.

1. Jesus' Prophetic Insight and Heart Discernment

"*Jesus answered, 'A person who has bathed does not need to wash, except for his feet, but is completely clean. And you are clean, but not every one of you.'*" – John 13:10

Before betrayal even occurred, Jesus demonstrated prophetic insight. He knew who would fail Him—and still chose to serve them.

Peter's Heart: Clean But Flawed

In John 13, Peter resists Jesus' foot washing at first, misunderstanding the act's spiritual significance. When Jesus explains its necessity, Peter responds with eager submission: "Not just my feet, but my hands and my head also!" (John 13:9). Jesus affirms Peter's spiritual condition by calling him "clean," even though He knows Peter will deny Him.

Leadership Insight #1: Create a Fail-Forward Culture.

Jesus modelled a leadership approach that anticipates failure and makes room for redemption. He prophesied Peter's denial and interceded for his restoration (Luke 22:31–32). Peter's betrayal was not born from malice, but from fear and weakness. His repentance opened the door to restoration. Leaders must develop the emotional maturity to disciple people through failure, not disqualify them because of it. Peter represents the leader, team member, or loved one who breaks trust but desires to be healed and restored. Their heart is teachable—even if their actions are painful.

Judas' Heart: Active, Present, but Distant

Judas, too, had his feet washed by Jesus. Yet Jesus said of him, "You are not all clean." Judas never called Jesus "Lord," only "Rabbi"—a telling sign of his disconnect (Matthew 26:25). Despite proximity, position, and power, Judas never truly submitted his heart.

Leadership Insight #2: Discern When to Say No.

Not everyone who works for you is walking with you. Judas looked the part, talked the part, and served in public ministry. Yet Jesus discerned that his heart was never with Him. We have a generation of people who heal the sick, cast out demons, and preach but do not relate to Jesus as Lord. Leaders must move beyond logic and titles, learning to rely on spiritual discernment. If someone consistently unsettles your spirit, seek godly counsel and act with wisdom. Discernment is not suspicion—it is protection. Judas represents the person whose motives are fundamentally misaligned. Restoration is not possible without repentance.

<u>2. Jesus' Love and Service to All</u>

"*Having loved His own who were in the world, He loved them to the end.*" – John 13:1

What's most astonishing is that Jesus washed Judas' feet, knowing he would betray Him within hours. He didn't humiliate him. He didn't isolate him. He served him.

Leadership Insight #3: Extend Unconditional Love Without Unwise Access.

Mature leaders can treat Judas and John with the same dignity. While not everyone deserves intimate access to your life, everyone should experience the grace of your leadership. This doesn't mean enabling betrayal—but it does mean leading with love, even when your heart is heavy.

3. Jesus' Restoration and Response

After His resurrection, Jesus reinstates Peter not with shame but with questions of love:

"*Simon, son of John, do you love Me?*" ... "*Then feed My sheep.*" – John 21:15–19

Peter's restoration came after repentance and was built on love for Jesus. His failure didn't disqualify him—it refined him.

Leadership Insight #4: Restore the Repentant.

Restoration must always be a possibility for the truly repentant. Galatians 6:1 instructs us to restore gently, not harshly. The fruit of repentance—humility, change and cooperation—is key. Restoration is not about returning someone to their previous position, but about relational and spiritual reconciliation.

Judas' End: Remorse Without Repentance

Judas felt regret, but he never returned to Jesus. Instead, he returned the silver and ended his own life. Remorse is not repentance. Regret without transformation does not lead to restoration.

Leadership Insight #5: No Repentance, No Restoration.

Tears are not always a sign of change. Restoration requires fruit—actions, not just emotions. Leaders must be courageous enough to close the door when necessary. You are not obligated to reconcile with someone who refuses to repent.

The Leadership Ultimatum: Betrayal Is Inevitable

Leadership will expose you to betrayal. Some relationships will be painfully ended. Others will be painfully restored. Regardless of the outcome, here are key reminders:

- Love deeply—but place your full trust in God.
- Discern wisely—not every person is meant to stay.
- Lead redemptively—because restoration is part of your legacy.

Jesus shows us how to lead through betrayal with wisdom, grace, and courage. The question is not whether you will face betrayal—but how you will respond when you do.

Grace in Action: Restoring Without Regret

When Derrick first came to the ministry, it was clear he had strong leadership potential—vision, confidence, and charisma. Over time, however, it became apparent that some of his interpersonal interactions left people feeling injured, unheard or discouraged. I addressed the concern directly, knowing that part of leadership development involves honest conversations about impact, not just intention.

Although his initial response seemed fine, it wasn't clear if the message landed and he truly took it to heart. I decided to continue investing in his growth, offering prayer, counsel, and leadership opportunities. Then, at one point, it was brought to my attention that he had spoken critically of me to someone else in the congregation.

That moment was deeply disappointing—not because of the opinion itself, but because trust had been damaged in a relationship where I had chosen to stand with someone through challenges. I addressed it clearly and set firm boundaries, deciding to watch for change over time rather than react quickly.

To Derrick's credit, I began to notice a genuine shift—his posture softened, his communication improved, and he began speaking openly about how grace had impacted him. He would often tell others, "I didn't deserve the second chance I got, but I was given one—that's why I lead differently now.". This experience reinforced something I believe deeply: restoration is never risk-free, but when it's grounded in repentance and guided by discernment, it can produce transformation and even testimony. Grace doesn't mean avoiding boundaries—it means applying them in a way that creates room for growth.

Release Without Regret: When Grace Has Boundaries

I once mentored Lucy for years—investing time, resources, and guidance to help her grow personally, spiritually, and in leadership. So when I was contacted by her pastor, I was blindsided. He shared that Lucy had been speaking negatively about me. The pastor was saddened because it was clear that it was a power play. He said, "It's sad how people can be so fickle." The pain wasn't just in what was said—it was in who said it.

Months later Lucy suddenly reached out in a seemly friendly tone—almost as though nothing had happened. I prayed, and I sensed the Holy Spirit leading me to confront the situation with grace and truth. When I raised the issue, the response was surface-level—expressing regret for how I "felt," but taking no true ownership of her actions. I was stunned. Weeks passed. She reached out again, expressing "deep respect" and a wish to reconnect—but again, without any acknowledgement of the betrayal or taking any responsibility. It became clear: there was no repentance, only remorse for the discomfort of being confronted.

I also realised I had seen signs of this behaviour before—just not directed at me. I had even addressed it in the past, but now I was on the receiving end. It helped me see patterns I had missed, reflect on what criteria qualifies access and the importance of slowing down before entrusting certain roles to people. So I responded clearly, calmly and respectfully. I let Lucy know I appreciated the sentiment, but her actions had already spoken. I explained that no further conversation was needed—not out of malice, but out of respect for the boundary her choices had drawn. I would not betray my right to emotional health by preserving a relationship that no longer honoured mutual respect, genuine love and ownership. Lucy was shocked. But I had peace. I believe she expected a "pastoral" or passive response—but not this time. This time, I didn't respond from a place of guilt or fear—especially not the fear of abandonment. I responded from freedom. And it was one of the clearest signs of wholeness in my leadership journey. Leadership Lesson: Sometimes protecting what God has restored in you means refusing to reopen a door that broken trust—without genuine repentance—has already closed.

Leadership Insight #6: Discern When Peace Requires Distance

There comes a point where, as leaders, we must protect the emotional and spiritual health God has restored in us. Grace is not the absence of boundaries; it includes them. Grace and restoration are not the same thing. Forgiveness is commanded, but access must be discerned. Leadership maturity includes the courage to end relationships that are corrosive to your calling. Lucy's lack of accountability made it clear that while forgiveness was possible, restoration was not. As painful as it is, there are relationships that disqualify themselves from full restoration—not because of their failure, but because of their refusal to acknowledge it. We are not called to be perpetual emotional martyrs for people unwilling to change. This is where discernment must triumph over guilt or sentiment. Sometimes leadership looks like closing a door gently, but firmly, and choosing peace over prolonged dysfunction.

Leadership Warning: Praise and Criticism Are Both Dangerous Without Perspective

Leaders, I must also give a clear warning. Do not let the praise go to your head, and do not let the criticism go to your heart. Praise can be a sedative that numbs our discernment, and criticism can be a dagger that pierces our identity if we're not rooted in Christ. If you build your confidence on applause, you'll collapse under accusation. This is why our ultimate trust must remain anchored in God—not in people, popularity, or even outcomes. Remember: The same crowd that shouted "Hosanna!" on Sunday was shouting "Crucify Him!" by Friday. The people who once celebrated Jesus turned on Him in a matter of days. Not because He changed—but because He didn't conform to their expectations. That moment in Jesus' journey is a sobering reminder for us: public approval is not the same as divine affirmation.

Leadership Insight #7: Anchor Your Identity in the Father, Not in the Applause

Your validation must come from Heaven, not human praise. Whether honoured or hated, Jesus remained secure because His identity was rooted in His relationship with the Father. That same security is available to you. If you are easily flattered, you will be easily manipulated. Stay grounded in God. Let praise pass through you and return it to God. Let criticism be filtered through truth and grace. And in both, remain anchored in who God says you are.

When You Are the Betrayer

It's one thing to talk about those who have betrayed you—but what about when you're the one who's broken someone's trust? I've had to face difficult moments where my own actions—whether careless or reactive—did not reflect the values I hold dear. In one particularly difficult season, I made choices that brought disappointment and pain to those who were relying on me for truth, love, and integrity. Their feelings of hurt and mistrust were valid. I had to humble myself—through intentional conversations, meetings, and letters—to apologise sincerely. Some relationships were rebuilt. Others were not. I respect both outcomes. One of the most sobering moments came during a conversation with my spiritual mother, Dr. Sharon. She told me, "Emmanuel, as a leader, you carry greater weight. Sometimes some people will never see how they betrayed you—but you must own your part, find the testimony in it, learn and move on. That's the weight of leadership." She was right. I learned that telling your side of the story isn't always the highest priority—it can sometimes get in the way of the deeper work of personal growth.

As a leader, I've learned that our decisions carry disproportionate weight. When someone hurts a leader, the leader is expected to forgive and move on. But when a leader hurts someone, that pain is amplified—because the position carries greater influence, trust, and spiritual weight. This doesn't mean leaders should be shamed or held hostage to guilt. But it does mean we must take full ownership of how our role magnifies the impact of our behaviour. Trust is earned in ounces but lost in tons. The lessons I learned in that season were painful, but I do not carry them in shame. I carry them as wisdom. They have become sacred teachers—faithful enough to mark me and wise enough to reshape me. They are a reminder that leadership is not about being above failure—it's about being willing to own your failures quickly, fully, and humbly.

I share this not to glorify failure, but to offer a warning:

- Be mindful of the weight you carry.
- Handle people with care.
- Live and lead with humility.
- And when you get it wrong—own it.

God's mercy is still available. Healing is still possible. But it begins with truth.

How to Repair Trust

I want you to know there is hope. This chapter will not end in despair but with a promise of redemption. I've seen dead relationships resurrected. Marriages, friendships, families, and even ministries-restored to the glory of God. Trust can be repaired. But it takes intentionality, effort, humility, and cooperation from everyone involved. The following keys to rebuilding trust are adapted from the wisdom of Mark Laaser (1996, pp. 74-77). They are not just steps-they are heart postures that help position a broken relationship for restoration.

1. Christ-Centred

At the core of trust, restoration is a Christ-like attitude toward one another. This means choosing to see the other person through the lens of Jesus-not just through the hurt, betrayal, or disappointment. This also requires sincere, non-manipulative prayer. When possible, pray together. There's something deeply transformative that happens when two people unite in prayer, especially in the context of a marriage that has been wounded by betrayal. Jesus is the only one who can truly mend hearts.

2. Committed

There are times in life when we must commit before we feel like it. Rebuilding trust often begins as a decision of the mind, long before it becomes a feeling of the heart.

You may not feel trust yet. But you can choose to show up for the process. Commitment means being willing to engage emotionally, spiritually, and practically-even when it's uncomfortable or slow. This signals to all parties involved that rebuilding the relationship is worth the effort.

3. Continuing

Sometimes when a person repents, they want to be trusted immediately. They may even quote Scripture about forgiveness to speed the process along. But this is neither fair nor realistic. Broken trust takes time to heal. With God's grace and support, healing will come-but it is a process. The person who has been hurt is grieving the loss of trust, and grief has no set timeline. Don't rush it. Trust is earned over time, not demanded in a moment.

4. Communicating

Trust thrives in honesty-and is destroyed by secrecy. When communication breaks down, trust begins to decay. You must create space to talk. Develop practical strategies for expressing feelings honestly and safely. For some, shame has led to secrecy: "If they knew the real me, they wouldn't love me." That lie keeps people silent and causes more damage. Telling the truth-especially about painful or sinful things-can be frightening. But when done wisely and with love, it can also be incredibly healing.

A few essential guidelines:

- Never tell the truth just to punish the other person.
- Never tell the truth to manipulate someone into forgiving you.
- Never weaponise truth that's been shared in vulnerability.

Trust is built when truth is spoken in love and handled with care.

5. Consistent

Rebuilding trust doesn't happen through words-it happens through patterns.

If you say you will change, your behaviour must reflect that-consistently, over time. Actions must align with words. Emotional reliability, follow-through, and personal accountability all matter. Consistency brings stability. And stability makes trust possible again.

6. Considerate

If your actions-whether sinful, careless, or negligent-damaged someone else, you must walk gently with them as they heal.

Here's what that looks like:

- Don't expect them to "get over it" quickly.

- Accept that current events may trigger old pain.
- Be willing to listen to how your actions hurt them, even if it happened long ago.

You cannot demand trust while being dismissive of their wounds. Consideration is active empathy. It's compassion in motion.

7. Control Surrendered

Rebuilding trust is a lot like salvation-it begins with surrender.

We must release control. We cannot force someone to love us, to stay, or to forgive. That must come from their heart, not our pressure. Surrender also means letting go of the illusion that we can manage outcomes. Whether in marriage, friendship, or ministry, we must be willing to say: "Lord, I place this person, this relationship, this process, in Your hands." Sometimes, to truly restore a relationship, we must be willing to lose it first. You can't force someone into loving you. You can only surrender them to God, who does the deeper work. Rebuilding trust will stretch you. It may break you open in ways you didn't expect. But if you stay Christ-centred, committed, and surrendered, you will not only see restoration-but you'll be transformed by it. There is hope. God is a redeemer of time, truth, and trust.

Conclusion: Betrayal, Trust, and the Leader's Heart

Rebuilding trust is not only possible—it is powerful. I have regained the trust of those I once wounded. I've also extended trust again to those who betrayed me. In both directions, the process was not easy—but it was sacred. Trust, at its core, is an attitude. It's a posture of surrender—

of releasing people, pain, and outcomes into the hands of a just and sovereign God. As leaders, we are called to walk in both wisdom and grace: discerning who to trust, and when; but also learning to love people through the eyes of Christ, not through the lens of betrayal. Leadership will expose the cracks in your character—but it will also give you space to be healed. Betrayal may break your heart, but it doesn't have to break your future. When trust is rebuilt with humility and truth, it can birth a deeper love, honour, and respect than what existed before. My prayer is that God gives you the courage to confront betrayal honestly, the humility to own your failures, the strength to set healthy boundaries, and the grace to hope again. May He give you discernment for who to trust—and healing and repair to the relationships He has ordained in your life. You are not called to lead perfectly. But you are called to lead from a whole heart. And even after betrayal—your heart can be whole again.

Chapter 10 reflections: The Wounds of Betrayal: Leading through Pain

Memory Verse

'You intended to harm me, but God intended it for good to accomplish what is now being done, the saving of many lives.' - Genesis 50:20

Personal Reflection Questions

1. Have I experienced betrayal in my leadership journey? How did I respond—emotionally, spiritually, relationally?
2. Are there areas where I still carry wounds from broken trust? Have I brought these to God for healing?
3. Have I been the one who betrayed someone else's trust? Have I taken full ownership of my actions, or hidden behind justifications?
4. What relationships may need boundaries, restoration, or release in this season?
5. Am I learning to see others—not through the lens of disappointment—but through the eyes of Christ?
6. What does rebuilding trust look like for me practically—with God, with others, and with myself?
7. Am I willing to do the deep work required to lead from a whole and honest heart?

Closing Prayer

Father, Thank You for being close to me in every moment of pain, betrayal, and confusion. Heal the parts of my heart that have been wounded and give me wisdom where trust has been broken. Help me to own where I've fallen short, and to extend grace where it's needed. Teach me how to lead with love, humility, and courage. May I not be hardened by betrayal but refined by it—and may I reflect You more with every step forward. In Jesus' name, Amen.

Chapter 11

Jesus Had Boundaries—Why Don't You?"

Access Is a Real Thing

When I think back over the different seasons of ministry I've walked through, one image often comes to mind—Jesus moving through the crowds, surrounded by people pressing in, reaching out, brushing against Him. And then He stops and asks, *"Who touched Me?"* (Luke 8:45). The disciples are baffled— "Master, the people are crowding and pressing against you." But Jesus knew someone had touched Him differently—deliberately—drawing power from Him. That moment has always struck me because it reveals something profound: not all access is the same. In ministry, in leadership, in life—access is real. Many people may be drawn to you, but not all want *you*—most are drawn to what you carry. Coming to terms with that truth was one of the most sobering yet transformative shifts in my journey. I say this to you in love and honestly: most people do not care about you personally; they care about your anointing, your wisdom, your gifting, your presence and your time. And if you don't grasp that, you'll live drained, misunderstood, and misaligned.

Studying Jesus' life through the lens of boundaries changed everything for me. I realised—sometimes with deep conviction—how often He made space to withdraw, to say no, to refuse to be driven by the urgency of others. He didn't allow neediness to dictate His obedience. I had to process this with mixed emotions: gratitude for the boundaries I now live by, but also forgiveness toward myself for the times I hadn't stewarded access well—for letting guilt or fear of being misunderstood keep me from saying no. But here's what I thank God for: I am not in that place anymore. His grace and His Spirit have empowered me to live and lead from a much stronger, and more secure place now. I no longer confuse people's admiration for genuine care, nor do I mistake being needed for being valued. I write this not as theory, but as someone walking in the reality of it today. Because if you don't define your boundaries, your assignment will be at the mercy of everyone else's agenda. And if you don't steward access well, you'll confuse being needed with being valued.

Jesus modelled a leadership marked not only by compassion and availability, but by clarity and conviction in His use of boundaries. Throughout the Gospels, we see Jesus withdrawing from crowds, saying "no" to demands, protecting His time with the Father, and refusing to let people—or even close friends—determine the direction of His ministry. For leaders today, embracing healthy boundaries is not a sign of weakness but a strategic, Spirit-led discipline and even warfare. Boundaries are not barriers to ministry—they are safeguards for your calling, your intimacy with God, and your capacity to sustain long-term Kingdom impact. Without boundaries, access becomes diluted, influence becomes fragmented, and calling is compromised. To protect your purpose, you must steward your energy, your time, and your emotional space with wisdom. If Jesus, fully God and fully man, lived with intentional limits, how much more must we do so as leaders entrusted with His mission? In this chapter, we will explore several boundary principles that can be discerned from the life of Christ. These principles—spiritual, emotional, physical, relational, financial, directional, and missional—reveal how Jesus led with holy restraint and divine focus. Each principle offers practical insight for leaders seeking to follow Jesus' example in stewarding access, protecting vision, and maintaining alignment with the Father's will.

1. <u>Jesus Withdrew to Pray</u>

Scripture: *"Jesus often withdrew to lonely places and prayed."* — Luke 5:15–16

Implication: Leaders must protect personal time with God. Constant output without input leads to burnout. Your spiritual authority flows from your private devotion, not your public platform.

Leadership Lesson:

Solitude is not selfish—it's sacred. Prioritising time alone with God fuels long-term leadership effectiveness. Leaders who fail to retreat eventually collapse. You cannot lead from a dry well.

Practical Ways to Set This Boundary:

- Schedule time with God like a non-negotiable meeting. Put prayer and Bible reading in your calendar.
- Create digital boundaries. Turn off devices during devotional times to protect focus.
- Communicate clearly. Let your team or family know when you are unavailable for prayer and renewal.
- Find your quiet place. Identify a consistent space (even a walk or parked car) where you meet with God.
- Start small, stay consistent. A short, focused time daily builds spiritual stamina over time.

2. Jesus Set Boundaries to Rest and Recharge

Scripture:

"The apostles gathered around Jesus and reported to him all they had done and taught. Then, because so many people were coming and going that they did not even have a chance to eat, he said to them, 'Come with me by yourselves to a quiet place and get some rest.' So they went away by themselves in a boat to a solitary place." — Mark 6:30–32

Context:

After an intense season of ministry, Jesus observed the physical and emotional toll it had taken on His disciples. Instead of allowing the demands of the crowds to continue dictating their pace, He initiated a pause for solitude and rest.

Implication:

Jesus modelled the importance of rhythm, rest, and healthy disengagement—even when there was still more work to do. He did not let people's expectations rob His team of renewal. Leisure and stillness were not a luxury; they were essential to sustainable ministry.

Leadership Lesson:

Leaders must take initiative to protect time for rest. Constant busyness is not always obedience—it can be avoidance or burnout in disguise. Boundaries around leisure are not selfish; they're stewardship. If Jesus made time to withdraw and recharge, leaders must do the same to avoid leading on empty.

Practical Ways to Set This Boundary:

- Schedule regular sabbath days. Block off one day per week for rest, reflection, and no ministry activity.
- Create non-negotiable "off" times. Establish clear hours in your week when you're unavailable for meetings, emails, or pastoral duties.
- Build margin into your calendar. Avoid back-to-back commitments. Leave space to breathe, pray, and recover.
- Take retreats seriously. Set time aside quarterly or biannually to get away alone or with a mentor/partner/friend to recharge.
- Say "no" without allowing guilt to steer you. Decline good opportunities if they compromise your rest and well-being—your "yes" is only as strong as your boundaries.
- Rest with God, not just from work. Use rest periods to reconnect spiritually, not just to catch up on sleep or entertainment.

3. <u>Jesus refused to let His Disciples determine the direction of His Mission</u>

Scripture:

"Peter took Him aside and began to rebuke Him. 'Never, Lord!' he said. 'This shall never happen to you!' Jesus

turned and said to Peter, 'Get behind me, Satan! You are a stumbling block to me; you do not have in mind the concerns of God, but merely human concerns.'" — Matthew 16:21–23

Context:

After Jesus revealed to His disciples that He must suffer and die, Peter—out of love but misunderstanding—tried to deter Him. Jesus immediately confronted the interference, even calling it satanic in origin, because it attempted to redirect Him from the cross.

Implication:

Though Peter was a close friend and key disciple, Jesus did not allow emotional closeness to override spiritual conviction. He set a clear verbal and ideological boundary: His mission would not be reshaped by well-meaning but misaligned voices. Even well-meaning friends may project their fears or expectations onto your calling. Leaders must filter advice—even from inner-circle voices—through the lens of obedience to God. Sentiment cannot override assignment.

Leadership Lesson:

Even trusted inner-circle relationships can unintentionally become obstacles. Leaders must courageously protect the direction God has given them, even if it means confronting or correcting close allies. Love does not eliminate the need for clarity and alignment.

Practical Ways to Set This Boundary:

- Clarify your assignment. Regularly revisit what God has specifically called you to do, so you can easily identify misalignment—even from well-meaning voices.
- Use clear language. When someone's influence begins to shift your focus, lovingly but firmly redirect with phrases like, *"That's not the direction the Lord has given me."*
- Correct the misalignment and ground your answer in scripture. What you tolerate will dominate. Be willing to let people walk away.
- Create accountability for your mission. Surround yourself with people who will call you deeper into your calling—not away from it.
- Don't over-explain obedience. Sometimes clarity will offend. Resist the urge to defend what God has told you to do when others don't understand it.
- Discern spirit over sentiment. Ask, *"Is this counsel rooted in faith or fear? In revelation or reaction?"*—and respond accordingly.
- Establish emotional boundaries. Don't let closeness or loyalty pressure you into compromise. Stay anchored to purpose, not just relationships.
- Set Expectations with Your Inner Circle. Communicate that while input is valued, you are ultimately led by the Spirit and Scripture—not just opinions or personal comfort. Build a culture where trusted team members know they are stewards of vision, not owners of it—

empowering them to support rather than steer the mission.

When Their Vision Wasn't *The* Vision

Early in my leadership journey, shortly after launching a ministry project I knew God had placed on my heart, a few experienced and passionate people joined the team. Their energy was encouraging, and I valued their input. But it soon became clear that our sense of direction was not the same. They had strong ideas about what the ministry should focus on, and their vision began to pull in a different direction from the one God had entrusted to me.

At first, I wrestled with whether I was being too rigid. I even entertained some of their ideas. But over time, I began to feel a tension in my spirit—an inner check that I was no longer running with the vision God had given me. In prayer, I heard the Holy Spirit say, "You can't lead people to the vision I gave you if you let others rewrite it." I met with them and, with respect, clarified the assignment. I explained that while ideas and creativity were welcome, the foundation of the mission and vision God gave me was not up for negotiation. They didn't receive it well, and eventually, they chose to leave. It was painful, but necessary.

That season taught me a truth I still carry today: agreement is not the same as alignment. Even well-meaning, gifted people can unintentionally dilute or divert your mission if they aren't walking in step with it. As a leader, your responsibility is not just to gather people—but to guard the vision. Leadership Lesson: Protecting the vision may cost you relationships, but losing the vision will cost you your calling.

4. Jesus Maintained Boundaries with the Samaritan Woman at the Well

Scripture:

"His disciples had gone into the town to buy food. The Samaritan woman said to Him, 'You are a Jew and I am a Samaritan woman. How can you ask me for a drink?'... He told her, 'Go, call your husband and come back.'" — John 4:4–26

Context:

Jesus engaged in a deeply meaningful conversation with a Samaritan woman—crossing cultural, ethnic, and gender boundaries—but He did so with great intentionality and purity. When the conversation touched personal and intimate matters, Jesus redirected the focus to her life situation, not to emotional entanglement.

Implication:

Jesus engaged with respect, clarity, and purpose. He neither avoided women nor blurred emotional lines. His boundary was set by truth and mission, not cultural fear or inappropriate familiarity.

Leadership Lesson:

Leaders must interact with the opposite sex with spiritual discernment, emotional wisdom, and clear purpose. Avoiding necessary interactions out of fear is not healthy, but neither is allowing closeness that confuses roles or

necessary for the work at hand. Rather than allow any potential for misunderstanding, I decided to set a clear and healthy boundary early. I redirected our communication through team channels and included others in relevant conversations. I also ensured that any in-person interactions took place in public or group settings connected to ministry purposes. She respected the boundary, and in the long run, it strengthened mutual trust and safeguarded the working relationship. It also gave her space to continue serving with clarity and confidence, without unnecessary distractions or confusion.

Leadership takeaway: Boundaries set early are not about shutting people out—they're about keeping everyone safe. Healthy boundaries preserve integrity, foster trust, and create space for ministry to thrive without the risk of blurred lines.

5. <u>Jesus Challenged Toxic Expectations</u>

Scripture:

After feeding the 5,000, Jesus confronted the crowd: "You are looking for me, not because you saw the signs but because you ate the loaves and had your fill." — John 6:26

Context:

Jesus had just performed a powerful miracle—feeding thousands with limited resources. The crowd followed Him afterward, not out of spiritual hunger, but because they wanted more physical provision. Rather than being flattered or manipulated by their pursuit, Jesus exposed their true motives.

Implication:

People will come to you for what they can get from you—your gifts, your position and your resources. Jesus lovingly challenged the crowd's superficial motivations and refused to shape His ministry around consumer expectations. As a leader, you must lovingly challenge unhealthy dependencies and refuse to be manipulated by people's needs or praise.

Leadership Lesson:

Healthy leadership means refusing to feed entitlement or enable dependency. Just because people praise you doesn't mean they value your purpose. Leaders must learn to lovingly confront misplaced expectations and anchor their identity in God's assignment—not people's applause. You are called to serve people, not be controlled by them.

Practical Ways to Set This Boundary:

- Clarify expectations early. Whether it's in ministry, mentorship, or leadership roles, define what you are (and aren't) there to provide.
- Discern motives. Ask, *"Is this person hungry for truth or just for benefits?"* Let your discernment—not people's enthusiasm—guide your engagement.
- Say no without guilt. Jesus wasn't afraid to turn away from the crowd. Not every need is your assignment.

Learn to say, *"That's not something I can provide right now."*

- Teach people to seek God, not just your gift. Redirect their dependence by pointing them to Scripture, prayer, and personal growth—not just access to you.
- Don't perform for approval. Monitor your own heart—are you doing this to please God or gain applause? Re-align when necessary.
- Regularly review your boundaries. Crowds may grow, but your margin must remain guarded. If demand increases, so must your discernment.

6. <u>Jesus Set Financial Boundaries</u>

Scripture:

"Someone in the crowd said to him, 'Teacher, tell my brother to divide the inheritance with me.' But he said to him, 'Man, who made me a judge or arbitrator over you?' And he said to them, 'Take care, and be on your guard against all covetousness, for one's life does not consist in the abundance of his possessions.'" — Luke 12:13–15

Context:

A man approached Jesus with a financial dispute, expecting Him to intervene and resolve a family inheritance issue. Jesus refused to get entangled in personal financial affairs that were outside the scope of His calling.

Implication:

Jesus set a clear boundary around financial expectations placed on Him. He didn't allow people to pull Him into disputes or make Him responsible for fixing their money issues. Instead, He redirected the conversation toward the heart—addressing covetousness rather than cash.

Leadership Lesson:

Leaders are often expected to solve other people's financial problems or take on burdens not assigned to them. Jesus modelled that it's okay to say, "That's not my role." You are not obligated to become the financial saviour of others. Boundaries protect your emotional capacity and keep you aligned with your true assignment.

Practical Ways to Set This Boundary:

- Clarify your role early. Let people know up front that you're not responsible for mediating financial disputes or providing personal financial rescue.
- Refer, don't rescue. Point individuals to professional, legal, or pastoral resources rather than trying to resolve everything yourself.
- Watch for guilt traps. People may use emotional or spiritual pressure ("you're a leader," "God would want you to help")—stay rooted in discernment, not demand.
- Protect personal finances. Don't loan or give under emotional pressure. Create a personal policy on when and how you give financially.

- Shift focus to the heart. Like Jesus, redirect conversations from money to motive—what's driving the request? Entitlement? Greed? Lack of stewardship?
- Use boundaries in conversation. Responses like *"I'm not the right person to make that decision,"* or *"That's outside my area of responsibility,"* create clarity and guard your peace.

Spirit-Led Generosity, Not Social Obligation

Misha and Jordan were warm, friendly, and eager to see God move. They had a real heart for community and were quick to connect with people. At the same time, I began to notice patterns that made other people—and myself—feel a subtle pressure or sense of obligation to meet their needs. Because I value generosity, I gave freely where I could, but I also recognised that true generosity must be Spirit-led, not driven by social pressure or unspoken expectations. Over time, I felt a nudge from the Holy Spirit to pause and prayerfully re-evaluate. I decided to have a gracious but honest conversation with them about attitudes toward resources and the importance of stewardship. Unfortunately, the response showed that there wasn't a readiness to embrace that change. To preserve the relationship and avoid unnecessary strain, I set clear boundaries and released any false sense of obligation I was carrying. I stopped giving out of guilt.

Leadership takeaway: Compassion and generosity are powerful Kingdom tools—but they must be paired with discernment. Spirit-led giving builds people up. Pressure-driven giving can blur boundaries and drain leaders unnecessarily. Healthy boundaries protect both the giver and the receiver, keeping relationships rooted in freedom, not obligation.

7. Jesus Declined a King-Making Crowd

Scripture:

"They intended to come and make him king by force, but Jesus withdrew again to a mountain by himself." — John 6:14–15

Context:

After the miraculous feeding of the 5,000, the people were so impressed that they attempted to crown Jesus as a political king. But Jesus discerned their motives and refused to let public pressure define His assignment. Instead of embracing popularity, He withdrew to a place of solitude and communion with the Father.

Implication:

Popularity does not equal purpose. Jesus did not allow crowds—or even seemingly positive affirmations—to define or distract Him from the Father's mission. Leaders must be deeply rooted in identity and vision, or they will be shaped by the expectations of others. Sometimes the loudest applause is a trap in disguise.

Leadership Lesson:

Every leader will face moments where influence and visibility present the temptation to shift focus or expand into roles God never assigned. True leadership includes the strength to say “no” to good opportunities that aren’t *God* opportunities. Staying hidden when the crowd wants to elevate you is sometimes the holiest response.

Practical Ways to Set This Boundary:

- Anchor your identity in calling, not crowds. Don’t let public affirmation inflate your ego or redirect your mission. Return often to the last clear word God gave you.
- Pause before accepting roles, titles, invitations or gifts. When offered influence, visibility, or promotion, take time to pray and discern. Not every open door is from God.
- Practice strategic withdrawal. Like Jesus, withdraw from the noise to gain clarity. Build regular rhythms of retreat where the only voice you listen to is God’s.
- Ask yourself: “Am I being crowned by men or called by God?” Let this question guide your decisions when you're elevated or celebrated.
- Surround yourself with people who will challenge ego-driven ambition. Invite mentors and peers who are not impressed by your platform but concerned with your soul.
- Say no with conviction, not apology. Politely and firmly decline roles or opportunities that would take you off-course, even if they seem prestigious.

When Opportunity Isn't Obedience

The year before I planted my first church was one of the most disorienting seasons of my life. I had just transitioned from my previous church and was pursuing a master's degree. I knew God had called me to preach the gospel, but the strategy wasn't fully clear, and I was in deep need of support and wise counsel. During that time, a respected leader in the body of Christ—let's call him David—took a personal interest in my journey. He offered encouragement and guidance in a fatherly way, which I appreciated. In one of our conversations, I shared that I was carrying a vision from God but didn't feel fully ready to act on it yet. The vision was still forming, and I needed more time in prayer and discernment. David then suggested an alternative: that I consider launching a branch of his ministry, with financial support included. On the surface, it seemed like a generous offer—but as I prayed, something in my spirit felt unsettled. I eventually shared that I didn't feel peace about moving forward. He received my decision courteously, but our connection ended soon after.

Looking back, I'm thankful for the clarity God gave me. That moment reinforced a vital leadership truth: not every open door is a divine one. Opportunities can look attractive, but if they require you to compromise peace or calling, they're not worth the cost. Leadership takeaway: In ministry, motives can be mixed. People may genuinely want to help, or they may see you as an asset to advance their own vision. That's why discernment and prayer are essential. Guard your peace, seek wise counsel, and remember—what God has called you to build must be led by His Spirit, not by money, position, or pressure.

8. Jesus Set Boundaries on Communication

John 19:9–11 – "*He entered his headquarters again and said to Jesus, 'Where are you from?' But Jesus gave him no answer. So Pilate said to him, 'You will not speak to me? Do you not know that I have authority to release you and authority to crucify you?' Jesus answered him, 'You would have no authority over me at all unless it had been given you from above.'*"

Context:

During His trial, Jesus stood before Pilate, who demanded answers. Rather than defending Himself against every accusation, Jesus chose silence. When He did speak, it was purposeful and aligned with divine authority—not driven by pressure, fear, or a need to justify Himself.

Implication:

Jesus demonstrated that communication is not always owed to everyone. Silence can be a powerful, intentional boundary. He refused to be manipulated or baited into unnecessary conversation, especially when the other party's motives were misaligned or rooted in power dynamics.

Leadership Lesson:

Leaders must recognise that not every question deserves an answer, and not every conversation needs to be had. Discernment in speech—when to speak, what to say, and when to remain silent—is a mark of mature, wise leadership. Boundaries in communication protect your peace, your focus, and your ability to lead from a place of clarity rather than compulsion.

Practical Ways to Set This Boundary:

- Practice the pause. Don't feel pressured to respond immediately. Take time to reflect and pray before answering confrontational or emotionally charged messages.
- Use silence intentionally. Sometimes silence is the best response to manipulation, gaslighting, or passive-aggressive behaviour. Like Jesus, silence can expose motives.
- Clarify communication expectations. Let others know you may not respond outside of your work hours or will need time to consider before engaging in complex discussions.
- Limit access during sensitive seasons. In high-stakes or emotionally vulnerable times (like transitions, grief, or conflict), reduce public or open dialogue to trusted voices only.
- Redirect unhealthy dialogue. When conversations turn unfruitful or manipulative, kindly disengage or redirect. You can say, *"I don't believe this conversation is moving in a healthy direction. Let's revisit it when emotions have settled."*
- Don't justify obedience. If God has spoken or led you clearly, not everyone needs an explanation. Discern when to offer clarity and when to hold your peace.

9. <u>Jesus Cared for His "Sheep"</u>

John 10:14–15 - *"I am the good shepherd. I know my own and my own know me... and I lay down my life for the sheep."*

Context:

Jesus identifies His followers as "sheep"—those who recognise His voice and follow Him. He speaks of deep, sacrificial care for these ones, emphasising relational connection, trust, and responsiveness. He does not extend this same depth of energy to everyone, but rather focuses His most intimate efforts on those aligned with His mission.

Implication:

While Jesus loved all, He invested most intentionally in those who were willing to follow Him and grow. His closest relationships—like the disciples—were not perfect, but they were hungry, teachable, and loyal. He modelled what it looks like to wisely allocate emotional and spiritual resources to those who respond to His leadership.

Leadership Lesson:

Leaders must prioritise their time, energy, and heart for people who are teachable, obedient, and faithfully engaged. Not every voice needs equal access. Not every relationship should require equal investment. Stewardship includes being intentional about who you pour into—"sheep" are those entrusted to your pastoral care.

Practical Ways to Set This Boundary:

- Discern fruit, not just need. Invest most deeply in those who show hunger for growth, consistency in relationship, and openness to correction.
- Limit energy-drain dynamics. Set time limits or boundaries for conversations that consistently go in circles or ignore wise counsel.
- Create inner-circle clarity. Like Jesus with the 12 (and the 3), recognise levels of relational access and be clear about who's in your primary investment zone.
- Don't chase—call. Sheep respond to the shepherd's voice (John 10:27). If someone consistently resists direction, it may be a sign to shift your level of investment.
- Protect your capacity. You can't pour into everyone the same way. Make space for those who are eager to grow and walk with you—not just those who want your presence without your process.
- Say "no" to rescuing. Caring for sheep doesn't mean solving every problem for them. Empower them to hear God, follow Him, and own their journey.

10. <u>Jesus Set Boundaries with "Pigs"</u>

Matthew 7:6 - *"Do not give dogs what is holy, and do not throw your pearls before pigs, lest they trample them underfoot and turn to attack you."*

Context:

Jesus warned His followers not to offer sacred truths to those who have no reverence for them. “Pigs” in this passage represent individuals who devalue or aggressively reject what is precious and holy. Rather than being moved by the worth of the “pearls,” they trample them—and often retaliate.

Implication:

Jesus taught that truth is not only powerful but also precious—and it must be protected. Discernment is key in determining when and where to share deeper revelation or correction. Sometimes withholding is wisdom, not cowardice. Leaders must know when to pause, when to walk away, and when silence is more honouring than speech.

Leadership Lesson:

Leaders must steward truth and vulnerability with care. Pouring deep wisdom, correction, or counsel into unreceptive, combative, or mocking individuals often leads to emotional fatigue and spiritual backlash. Not every conversation is redemptive. Honour the message by honouring the moment—and the recipient's readiness.

Practical Ways to Set This Boundary:

- Pay attention to response patterns. If someone repeatedly mocks, twists, or dismisses your input, it’s time to pause deeper sharing.

- Resist pressure to over-explain. You don’t owe sacred wisdom to people unwilling to steward it. Silence can be more strategic than defence.
- Discern posture, not just proximity. Someone being close to you (e.g., on your team or in your circle) doesn’t mean they’re ready to receive your pearls.
- Redirect conversations. Shift the focus or exit gracefully when dialogue becomes argumentative, dismissive, or disrespectful.
- Set limits on correction. Avoid excessive rebuke in spaces where there’s no fruit of repentance. Jesus only explained further to those who leaned in.
- Guard your emotional capacity. Protect your inner life by refusing to be drawn into cycles of unfruitful debate or emotional volatility.
- Remember: Retreat is not rejection. Pulling back from “pigs” is not abandoning them—it’s acknowledging that transformation can’t be forced.

When I Shared Too Much, Too Soon

There was a time I felt to share something deeply personal—a vision God had placed on my heart and some of the prophetic words that had shaped my journey. I shared it with someone I considered a mature believer; someone I thought would understand and even pray with me about it. But instead of honouring what I’d shared, they responded with sarcasm and passive-aggressive comments like, “Well, let’s see if that actually happens,” or “That sounds a bit ambitious, don’t you think?” I walked away from that conversation feeling exposed, misunderstood, and even silly. Not because of what I shared but where it landed. I hadn't just shared an idea—I had shared a pearl, something sacred. And it was trampled on. The Holy Spirit later reminded me: "Even Jesus didn't reveal everything to everyone." There's a reason He said not to throw pearls before pigs—not to insult others, but to *protect what is holy*. Some hearts are not in a place to handle the weight of revelation, and if you don't steward what's sacred, others won't either.

Key Lesson: Discern who is safe before you share what is sacred. Oversharing with unspiritual or unsubmitted people is not vulnerability—it's misplaced trust. It drains virtue from you in a harmful way compared to the strength you receive when shared with the right people.

Now I test the soil before I sow the seed. I ask questions like:

- Is this person spiritually maturing enough to carry this?
- Do they celebrate what God is doing in others—or compete with it?
- Have they proven to be confidential, prayerful, and discerning?

11. <u>Jesus Exposed and Warned Against "Wolves" (Matthew 7:15)</u>

"Beware of false prophets, who come to you in sheep's clothing but inwardly are ravenous wolves."

Context:

Jesus warned His disciples about deceptive individuals who appear trustworthy—wearing the disguise of "sheep"—but are in fact spiritually dangerous. These “wolves” manipulate, exploit, and devour others under the guise of righteousness. Jesus did not just avoid them—He publicly called them out and taught His followers to remain vigilant.

Implication:

Love does not require naivety. Jesus modelled that discernment and confrontation are necessary for protecting the integrity of the community. When hidden agendas or character corruption are tolerated, the flock suffers. Boundaries are a form of spiritual defence—not rejection, but protection.

Leadership Lesson:

Leaders are called to be both shepherds and watchmen. Guarding people doesn’t only involve feeding and nurturing—it also means identifying and confronting danger. Whether in the form of false teaching, spiritual manipulation, or abusive leadership, “wolves” must be lovingly but firmly exposed and removed from influence. Tolerating toxicity in the name of grace destroys what grace is meant to restore.

Practical Ways to Set This Boundary:

- Create a culture of accountability. Make sure your leadership environment doesn’t reward charisma over character. Build systems that prioritise integrity and feedback.

- Trust your discernment—then act. If the fruit doesn't match the presentation, don't delay in asking hard questions or taking protective action.
- Address manipulation directly. If someone repeatedly uses guilt, control, flattery, or fear to get their way, confront it promptly and biblically.
- Establish and enforce access levels. Wolves thrive in unchecked spaces. Guard leadership platforms, mentoring roles, and influence channels.
- Listen to repeated concerns. If multiple trusted voices raise red flags about a person, take them seriously. God often confirms discernment through others.
- Protect the vulnerable. Prioritise the safety of the "flock" over the comfort of the offender. Removing someone may feel hard—but leaving them unchallenged can cause deeper harm.
- Name behaviour without being unnecessarily harsh. You don't have to attack someone's identity, but you must be honest about their impact.
- Remove quietly, if necessary, publicly if required. If a wolf is harming others, visible correction or removal may be necessary for the sake of clarity and healing.

Conclusion: Jesus Had Boundaries – Why Don't You?

Jesus was the most loving, powerful, Spirit-filled leader to ever walk the earth—and He had boundaries. Not because He lacked compassion, but because He carried purpose. He knew that saying "yes" to the Father's will meant saying "no" to manipulation, distraction, and misplaced expectations. He wasn't driven by people's needs, pressures, or praise—but by intimacy with the Father and clarity of mission. If Jesus needed boundaries to fulfil His calling, how much more do we? In this chapter, I've shared lessons from both wins and mistakes—real moments that shaped how I lead today. I'm grateful to say that, years later, I now carry strong boundaries in these areas. But it wasn't automatic—it took growth, practice, reflection, and some hard conversations. Too many leaders today are exhausted, emotionally entangled, or spiritually depleted—not because they lack gifting or anointing, but because they lack boundaries. Boundaries are not unloving—they are the framework through which love, clarity, and fruitfulness flow. They protect what is holy. They preserve your emotional health. They help to prioritise what truly matters. Let this be your reminder: You are not called to be everyone's saviour. You are called to obey God. You don't need to apologise for protecting what God has entrusted to you. Setting boundaries isn't selfish—it's stewardship. Boundaries aren't selfish—they're sacred. They protect your peace, preserve your calling, and make space for healthy, Spirit-led leadership. And when you lead like Jesus—with wisdom, discernment, and sacred restraint—you'll find greater peace, power, and longevity in your calling. I share these stories to encourage you: don't wait for burnout or regret to clarify what God is already highlighting. So, pause and ask: Where do your boundaries need strengthening? What are you tolerating that God never asked you to carry? Are you leading like Jesus—or performing for people? Jesus had boundaries. Why don't you? It's time to grow, review, and walk in the purpose God desires for you.

Chapter 11 Reflections: Jesus Had Boundaries – Why Don't You?

Memory Verse:

"Above all else, guard your heart, for everything you do flows from it."— *Proverbs 4:23*

Personal Reflective questions

1. Boundaries in Prayer and Rest

    - Do I believe rest is spiritual, or do I feel guilty stepping away from constant activity?
    - How often do I withdraw to be alone with God, not just to prepare for ministry but to be refreshed?

2. Boundaries with the King-Making Crowd *(John 6:14–15)*

    - Am I tempted to let popular opinion steer my calling?
    - Have I ever compromised my convictions to maintain approval?
    - Do I know when to withdraw from applause and realign with God's mission?

3. Boundaries in Communication *(John 19:9–11)*

    - Do I over-explain myself to avoid being misunderstood?

- Am I spending emotional energy trying to convince people who aren't listening with the right heart?
- Have I learned to discern when silence is wisdom?

4. Boundaries with "Sheep" (Teachable Followers) *(John 10:14–15)*
    - Who are the "sheep" God has entrusted to me?
    - Am I pouring the most into those who are hungry, teachable, and faithful?
    - Where am I spending energy on people God hasn't assigned me to?
5. Boundaries with "Pigs" (Misaligned Hearers) *(Matthew 7:6)*
    - Am I giving time, wisdom, or vulnerability to people who consistently trample it?
    - Where do I need to stop casting pearls where they're not received?
6. Boundaries with Finances and Manipulation *(John 12:3–8)*
    - Do I feel guilty when I say no to financial or ministry requests?
    - Am I discerning with financial generosity, or easily influenced by pressure?
    - Have I let the fear of how it looks override what the Spirit is saying?

7. Boundaries with the Opposite Sex *(John 4:4–26)*

- Do I maintain emotional and spiritual clarity in my interactions?
- Have I allowed any connections to become too casual, intense, or emotionally entangled?
- Am I utilising accountability proactively?

8. Boundaries with Disciples Who Want to Redirect the Mission *(Matthew 16:21–23)*

- Am I letting well-meaning voices steer me off course?
- Do I confront misalignment directly, or shrink back out of fear of relational tension?
- Who do I need to gently but clearly correct to stay faithful to the call?

Closing Prayer

Father thank You for the way Jesus modelled boundaries rooted in love, truth, and wisdom.

Teach me to lead like Him—with courage, clarity, and conviction. Expose any places where guilt, fear, or pressure are driving my decisions. Give me strength to say no when needed, grace to correct with love, and discernment to recognise who You've truly called me to pour into. I surrender my relationships, my leadership, and my rhythms to You. Help me walk in both compassion and holy boundaries. In Jesus' name, Amen.

Section 3 - Released: Mission & Impact

The Mission of the Leader, *Activation, Transition & Kingdom Impact*

Focus: Apostolic & Prophetic leadership, transition, activating prophetic identity and the kind of leaders God is raising.

Chapter 12

Laying Apostolic and Prophetic Foundations

Apostolic and prophetic leaders are foundational to the Church's mission, called to build, align, and speak truth with boldness, humility, and vision. There is much debate within the Church today about the specific roles and functions of apostles and prophets, particularly as described in the New Testament. Yet, beyond these debates, a clear revival is underway. Many are being stirred by the Spirit to step into apostolic and prophetic callings, answering God's invitation to lead, build, and speak into His Church in fresh and powerful ways. However, while this movement gains momentum, practical language and frameworks for understanding these roles remain underdeveloped. Many who sense this calling wrestle with what it means to function apostolically and prophetically in everyday ministry and leadership contexts. This chapter explores the vital importance of apostolic and prophetic leadership in the Church's life and mission. It will show how these roles serve as essential pillars—enabling individual believers and faith communities to align with God's purposes, form healthy structures, and effectively engage in the mission of God in the world. By understanding and embracing apostolic and prophetic foundations, the Church can experience greater clarity, unity, and impact as it builds the Kingdom of God here on earth.

The Importance of Apostolic and Prophetic Leadership

"*Having been built on the foundation of the apostles and prophets, Jesus Christ Himself being the chief cornerstone, in whom the whole building, being fitted together, grows into a holy temple in the Lord, in whom you also are being built together for a dwelling place of God in the Spirit.*" - Ephesians 2:20-22

Key Words:

- Built
- Foundation
- Apostle
- Prophet
- Cornerstone

Interpretation

The first word to examine is "built" - translated from the Greek 'epoikodomeō', meaning to build upon. This word is formed from two parts:

- Epi - meaning 'upon', 'on top of'
- oikodomeō - meaning 'to build',

Together, epoikodomeō conveys the idea of building with order and purpose (order first and then equipping after). Imagine constructing a building - you wouldn't put the roof where the floor belongs or place windows where the doors should be. It's not enough to have materials; they must be properly arranged and placed in their correct order. This same principle applies to the body of Christ. Every believer has a unique, God-given place, and it is crucial not only to be equipped but to discover and embrace that specific role for the health and growth of the whole Church. Being gifted and called is not enough. You must come into alignment with God's order.

The second word is "foundation", from the Greek 'themelios', meaning substructure. It derives from 'tithēmi', meaning to place. This highlights the importance of intentionality in ordering and positioning the building blocks. The foundation is the reference stone on which all else is established. Jesus is the foundation and reference for everything in the body of Christ. True apostolic and prophetic ministry is Christocentric in nature.

The third, and perhaps most critical word, is "apostle" - from the Greek 'apostolos', meaning an ambassador of the Gospel who is sent. It is derived from 'apo' meaning away and 'stello' meaning to send, place, or set something in its intended position. Apostolic ministry is fundamentally a sent and sending ministry - moving from place A to place B with the purpose of making place B reflect place A. I will explore this concept more deeply later in the chapter.

The fourth word is "prophet" - from the Greek 'prophetes', meaning an inspired speaker or foreteller. This term carries rich meaning and insight, which I will also unpack later in this chapter.

Finally, the fifth word is "cornerstone", translated from the Greek 'akrogōniaios', meaning the extreme corner. This word combines 'akron' meaning uttermost part or extremity, and 'gōnia' meaning' angle or corner. Again, Jesus is the cornerstone and reference for measuring everything in the body of Christ.

Application

For the Church to reach its fullest potential, it must be firmly established on a Christ-centred foundation. Those who respect apostolic and prophetic doctrines and embrace their mindset and function will be most effective in building and advancing the Kingdom of God. Remember, everyone has a place in this spiritual architecture. God desires you to understand and step into your divinely appointed position. Yet, order must come before equipping.

Templates for Apostolic and Prophetic Ministry Structure

An apostolic mindset is essential for the Church to fulfil God's mission and be all that she has been called to be. The focus of apostolic ministry is primarily on making disciples and advancing God's purposes—not merely on meeting people's immediate needs. To be clear, the needs of people are important, but God's needs must come first; this is the proper order. Whenever the needs of men are placed above God's will, the Church risks sliding into carnality and idolatry—even if outward manifestations of God's Spirit are still evident. Below, we explore two contrasting ministry templates: a human-centred model and a Christocentric model.

A Human-Centred Template

Exodus 32 presents three leaders—Aaron, Joshua, and Moses—positioned at different levels on Mount Sinai. Moses stood at the summit, Joshua in the middle, and Aaron at the base. This mountain can symbolise spiritual consecration and leadership focus. Moses, at the top, represents the apostolic and prophetic leader whose focus was on divine needs and God's will. Aaron, positioned at the bottom, became compromised by the immediate demands of the people.

Moses ascended the mountain with an apostolic and prophetic mindset, prioritising God's agenda over the fleshly desires of the people. Leaders who fail to consecrate themselves to God risk losing authority to address these desires effectively and may become consumed with meeting people's needs above God's will. A ministry structure centred on human needs prioritises people's desires and comfort over discerning and obeying God's will. It often becomes fuelled by intimidation or appeasement and tends to measure success by attendance or seating capacity rather than by sending capacity and kingdom impact.

A Christocentric Template

In Mark 6:36-44, Jesus demonstrates a Christocentric model of ministry that prioritises order before equipping. The distribution of bread to the multitudes began with Jesus, then flowed to the apostles, and only then to the people—who had to sit in the order established by apostolic leadership. This passage reveals that some of the greatest blessings and miracles God intends to pour out on His Church can only flow when there is submission to apostolic and prophetic order. The barrier to receiving God's blessings is often not spiritual warfare, but a lack of alignment and order. By order, we don't mean merely well-organised programs or punctual meetings. True order is operating in alignment with the chief cornerstone—Jesus Christ—and His apostolic and prophetic foundation.

Working in Partnership

Healthy and effective ministry flows from the collaborative partnership of all fivefold ministry gifts—apostles, prophets, evangelists, pastors, and teachers—working together to equip the saints and build up the body of Christ (Ephesians 4:11–13). Each gift carries a unique grace and function, and when they operate in mutual honour and unity, the Church becomes a mature, mission-focused community.

While every ministry gift is vital, Scripture repeatedly affirms the foundational partnership between apostles and prophets (Ephesians 2:20). The apostolic gift brings government, alignment, and structure; the prophetic gift brings foresight, revelation, and spiritual discernment. When these two gifts work in synergy, the Church is both ordered and inspired—grounded in truth yet sensitive to the movement of the Spirit. To be clear: though apostolic and prophetic are the subject of this chapter it's impossible for the church to function without the collaboration of pastors, evangelists and teachers.

In my experience, apostolic ministry—when not complemented by prophetic insight—can drift toward rigidity or an overemphasis on order. Structure without revelation risks becoming legalistic. Likewise, prophetic ministry without apostolic grounding can become unstable or lack sustainability. It is the healthy tension between these two gifts that keeps the Church aligned with both God's truth and His timing. As we move forward, we will now take a closer look at prophetic ministry—what it is, how it operates, and why it remains vital for discerning the heart and voice of God in today's Church.

Types of Prophetism

Understanding the distinction between biblical and non-biblical expressions of prophecy is essential for cultivating a Christ-centred prophetic ministry. Scripture outlines both godly and ungodly manifestations of the prophetic.

1. Israelite Prophetism (Biblical/Judeo-Christian)

This refers to prophecy that originates from God and is rooted in the covenantal relationship between God and His people. These prophets speak by divine revelation and operate within God's moral and spiritual order.

This form of prophecy:

- Excludes: Occultic or esoteric practices such as necromancy, magic, divination, and mystical ceremonies.
- Includes: the clear communication of God's will, purpose, and plans, often calling people to repentance and alignment with God's covenant.

A prophet is one who speaks under divine inspiration—an interpreter through whom the will of God is expressed. The definitions below are descriptive, not exhaustive.

Greek Meaning

- Greek word: *prophētēs* (*pro* = in advance, first; *phēnē* = to speak another's mind)
- Literal meaning: *One who speaks the mind of God in advance.*
- Key functions:

- Transmits God's mind and heart without diluting it.
- Announces things ahead of time.

Hebrew Words for Prophet

1. Nabiy – *An inspired person*
    - One who receives inspiration from God and declares it.
    - *Inspiration* (Latin: *inspirare*) means "in the Spirit."
    - Example: A person who hears from God and communicates it to others.
2. Naba – *To blow, as if inflating a balloon*
    - God breathes His mind into you, filling and expanding you.
    - This inspiration comes from within but must be vocalised. Growth happens as you respond to what God reveals.
    - Examples:
        - Samuel (1 Samuel 3) – Responded to the voice of God.
        - Jeremiah (Jeremiah 1:11) – Received and declared God's words.

Scripture: "Surely the Sovereign LORD does nothing without revealing His plan to His servants the prophets. The lion has roared—who will not fear? The Sovereign LORD has spoken—who can but prophesy?" — Amos 3:7–8

2. Non-Israelite Prophetism (Unbiblical/Occultic)

This refers to prophecy or spiritual insight that arises from sources other than the Holy Spirit. It often mimics or distorts the prophetic but draws from demonic or soulish power. Common in pagan cultures and sometimes in contemporary spiritual environments that reject Christ.

- Practices include: divination, omens, necromancy, trance-like states, enchantments, and spirit-medium activity.
- Hebrew Insight: The term *nachashim* (from *nachash*, "serpent") is linked to deceptive, snake-like speech. A voice that speaks in the spirit of the serpent (read Genesis 3).

A New Testament example is the slave girl with a spirit of divination (*python* spirit) who followed Paul and his team. Though accurate in speech, her source was demonic. Paul cast the spirit out (Acts 16:16–18). The Old Testament Parallel is Balaam — though he heard from God, his heart was compromised, and his gift became a tool of corruption (Numbers 22–24; 2 Peter 2:15). The key Insight is that it's not the accuracy of the prophecy that defines the authenticity of a prophet, but the direction it leads you toward—does it draw you to Christ or away from Him? (See Deuteronomy 13:1–3).

Impact of Apostolic and Prophetic Leadership on Ministry

Apostolic and prophetic leadership creates a culture where God's people are equipped, aligned, and empowered to thrive. At the heart of this leadership is the belief that the Church is not merely a gathering place, but a ministry training centre, with discipleship and spiritual formation at its core. When the apostolic and prophetic work together, order is established, equipping becomes intentional, and every believer is mobilised into mission.

Below are three essential ministry dimensions that are transformed under apostolic and prophetic leadership:

1. Discipleship: Cultivating Worshippers, Not Consumers

Discipleship under apostolic and prophetic oversight involves more than knowledge transfer-it is about transformation. Jesus said, "*If anyone would come after me, let him deny himself and take up his cross and follow me*" (Matthew 16:24).

True discipleship requires:

- Complete loyalty to Christ.
- Endurance in persecution.
- Self-denial as a lifestyle.

This kind of formation demands an environment where submission to God's will is the priority, and where teaching, healing, and deliverance are embraced. Apostolic and prophetic leaders train believers to become worshippers - people who live to honour God-rather than consumers seeking only personal fulfilment. Without this, discipleship devolves into self-centred Christianity.

2. Service: Stewarding Calling, Timing, and Location

Apostolic and prophetic leaders play a crucial role in activating and stewarding the calling of others. Their role in leadership is not to dominate, but to discern, develop, and deploy. This includes:

- Discerning the Calling

Apostolic and prophetic leaders help individuals identify their gifts and divine assignment. They create opportunities to serve while calling disciples to humble submission, not self-promotion. Like John the Baptist, who discerned and affirmed Jesus publicly, mature leaders recognise what God is doing in others and call it forth with integrity.

- Discerning the Timing

Timing protects the integrity of the call. Entering too soon can result in pride, burnout, or harm to others. Apostolic and prophetic leaders bring wisdom, counsel, and sometimes restraint-propelling the stagnant, while also slowing the premature. Patience and humility become marks of maturity under such leadership.

- Discerning the Location

The apostle Paul's missionary strategy changed as the Spirit redirected his journey (Acts 16:6-10). Prophetic revelation guards against rigid planning and helps believers discern the where of their calling. Apostolic and prophetic leadership equips the Church to follow the Spirit's leading, both locally and globally.

3. Missional Imagination: Seeing and Serving God's Redemptive Plan

One of the most powerful outcomes of apostolic and prophetic leadership is the cultivation of missional imagination-the Spirit-inspired ability to see what God is doing in the world and participate with Him in it. This kind of imagination expands the Church's vision and involves:

- Engagement with the needs and hopes of the local community.

- Partnerships with like-minded individuals, churches, and networks.
- Prayerful discernment of God's redemptive activity in the region.
- Vocation as ministry, where believers use their careers (medical, legal, entrepreneurial, educational, etc.) as platforms for service and transformation.

Apostolic and prophetic leaders encourage ambidextrous ministry-where believers, like Paul the tentmaker, can serve in the marketplace and in the Church with equal devotion.

<u>Personal Example: A Time I Was Sent Apostolically</u>

The first church I planted was not something I rushed into. In fact, God gave me the blueprint nearly five years before I ever started. Over those years, the Lord continued to reveal elements of the structure and purpose—things I knew were from Him—but deep in my spirit, I also knew the timing wasn't yet right.

I submitted what I was sensing to a trusted prophetic leader—someone with a proven voice and spiritual maturity. They confirmed what I already suspected: the revelation was accurate, but the timing was off. They encouraged me to wait, assuring me that when the time was right, God would provide unmistakable confirmation. Five years later, everything began to align. The sense of timing, assignment, and even the geographical location came together with clarity. What began as a simple discipleship program soon became the foundation for a thriving church plant. That one step of obedience led to thousands of lives being transformed.

Looking back, this journey deeply affirmed my belief in the need for apostolic and prophetic collaboration. The apostolic grace gives vision and structure, but the prophetic voice helps discern timing and spiritual atmosphere. It's not enough to be sent—you must be sent at the right time, to the right place, with the right preparation. This experience taught me that fulfilling God's mission requires both patience and partnership. It's not just about revelation, but about divine order, accountability, and being sent—not just going.

A Time I Helped Bring Order to a Ministry

I once received a call from a pastor in another country who had become a father figure to many believers in his nation. While his local church remained small—rarely exceeding a hundred people—his regional revival gatherings were drawing crowds of multitudes. This disparity left him frustrated and confused. He deeply loved his church but sensed that his assignment was shifting. He just didn't have the language for what was happening within him. He reached out for my counsel. As he shared, I began to discern and explain what was taking place. The apostolic grace on his life was seeking expression—it longed to pioneer and establish, to equip and mobilise. At the same time, the prophetic grace in him was discerning the spiritual climate and hunger across the region. It became clear that he was still trying to function in a pastoral model while carrying an apostolic and prophetic mandate. I encouraged him to consider appointing a trusted pastor to lead the local church while he stepped into a more apostolic oversight role. His time, energy, and anointing were needed to help the region align with the Spirit's activity, especially through intercession and strategic equipping. He bore strong witness to this. Not long after, I travelled to that nation and helped implement doctrinal teaching that brought clarity to the movement. We established apostolic and prophetic foundations that empowered both the church and the broader network. Many were mobilised, and the transformation was undeniable. The results spoke for themselves—momentum increased, prayer intensified, healings, deliverances, salvations and spiritual alignment took root. This experience taught me how apostolic and prophetic grace doesn't just grow churches—it stewards movements. It helps leaders move beyond internal conflict and step confidently into their God-given assignments. When we honour God's order, we become effective participants in His mission.

Conclusion

The apostolic and prophetic model of leadership goes far beyond titles or platforms—it's about cultivating a people who are aligned with God's order and equipped to live sent lives. Through discipleship, service, and missional vision, this model transforms the Church from a passive gathering into a mobilised body released into mission. This is by no means an exhaustive list of all the functions or impacts of apostolic and prophetic leadership. Not all are called to be apostles or prophets by office, but all of God's people are called to be apostolic and prophetic in nature and function. That is, every believer is called to be sent, to discern God's voice, and to live in alignment with His purposes in the world. Now the question comes to you: Will you take your place? Will you embrace the discipline of alignment and the call to be equipped—not just for personal growth, but to be part of something bigger than yourself? The Church cannot rise into her full potential until every part is doing its work (Ephesians 4:16). Your obedience matters. Your alignment matters. Your voice matters. Its time you to come get into Gods order!

Chapter 12 Reflections: Laying Apostolic and Prophetic Foundations

Memory Verse

"Having been built on the foundation of the apostles and prophets, Jesus Christ Himself being the chief cornerstone, in whom the whole building, being fitted together, grows into a holy temple in the Lord." —Ephesians 2:20–21

Personal Reflection Questions

1. Am I currently living with an apostolic and prophetic mindset, or am I primarily focused on comfort and personal needs?

2. Do I recognise the difference between being equipped and being in divine order? Have I allowed God to both prepare and position me?

3. Have I invited trusted apostolic or prophetic voices into my life to help me discern timing, location, and calling? Who are they?

4. What part of the fivefold ministry have I resisted or misunderstood, and how might embracing it bring greater alignment in my life and ministry?

5. Where have I witnessed disorder in my ministry or context, and how might God be calling me to help bring His order and structure?

6. Do I truly believe I have a place in God's plan? What is stopping me from taking my place fully?

Closing Prayer

Father, thank You for the wisdom of apostolic and prophetic leadership. Help me to see my life, calling, and ministry from Your perspective. Align my heart with Your order and equip me with the grace to build according to Your pattern. Show me where I am to serve, how I am to grow, and when I am to be sent. May I never settle for comfort when You are calling me to be courageous. I take my place today—not in striving, but in surrender. In Jesus' name, amen.

Chapter 13

Theology of Transition

The only thing that does change is change! Stewarding transition well is central to sustaining your calling, deepening intimacy with God, and undergoing the transformation necessary for long-term leadership. In Scripture, transition is never accidental—it is a divine process where God refines identity, strips self-reliance, and prepares leaders for greater authority. Those who embrace transition faithfully—like David, Joshua, and Elisha—are not just moved; they are made. Leadership in the Kingdom of God is not static. Every calling is shaped by seasons of transition—moments where what was familiar is stripped away, and the new has not yet fully formed. These in-between seasons are not merely delays or detours; they are sacred spaces of formation. For biblical leaders, the ability to steward transition marked the difference between rising into divine purpose or forfeiting it prematurely. David's years between anointing and coronation, Moses' wilderness exile, and Joseph's journey through betrayal and prison all illustrate this truth: transition is God's container for calling. For today's leaders, understanding the theology of transition is not optional. It is in transition that God matures character, reshapes perspective, and builds the spiritual infrastructure to sustain influence. When we submit to God's process in these seasons, transition becomes the very environment where intimacy with Him is deepened, and transformation takes root.

The Cross: A Foundation for a Theology of Transition

The Cross stands at the very centre of Christian faith, offering not only a clear soteriology—the doctrine of salvation—but also serving as a profound theological model of transition. In the Cross, we find the clearest expression of God's redemptive process of endings, liminal space, and new beginnings.

1. Endings: Death and Separation

The crucifixion of Jesus represents the ultimate ending—an ending marked by suffering, surrender, and the public loss of identity and position. On the Cross, Christ bore the weight of sin and willingly embraced the end of His earthly ministry, reputation, and even fellowship with the Father ("My God, My God, why have You forsaken Me?"). The Cross is a place of separation—from life, from comfort, from power, and from human approval. All leaders will face such endings when God calls them out of old assignments, identities, or systems.

The Cross represents an ending. For Jesus, it was the end of public ministry, popularity, relationships, and even life itself. In leadership, endings often come through:

- Losing your job or leadership position
- Team members leaving suddenly
- Moving to a new city or ministry assignment
- A key project failing or funding being cut
- A friendship or relationship ending

These moments feel like defeat, but in God's hands, they are sacred.

Characteristics of the 'Ending' Phase

The 'Ending' phase of transition is often the most painful and disorienting, yet it is essential for growth, transformation, and maturity. Before anything new can begin, something old must die, be released, or be redefined. In leadership, this may take many forms—stepping down from a role, losing a team member, experiencing a ministry or business failure, changing career, moving or sensing God asking you to release something you've built. This phase is often misunderstood or resisted, but it is a sacred space where God invites deeper surrender and reformation. Here are some characteristics associated with this phase.

1. Loss of Identity or Role

Leadership roles often become intertwined with personal identity. When that role is stripped away, it can feel like losing yourself.

- What it feels like: "Who am I without this position, business etc?"
- What's happening spiritually: God is separating your identity from your assignment. He is reminding you that your value is not in what you do or who is with you, but in who you are in Him.
- Biblical parallel: David running from Absalom; Peter denying Jesus and being restored.

God often removes titles or roles to remind us we are still chosen without them.

2. Grief and Disorientation

Endings often bring deep emotional pain. Even when an ending is necessary or right, it still hurts.

- What it feels like: Sadness, anger, numbness, confusion, or spiritual dryness.
- Why it matters: Grief is not weakness-it's evidence that you were invested. Disorientation means you are no longer clinging to a false sense of control, which makes space for dependence on God.
- Practical insight: Allow yourself time to grieve. You can't move on without acknowledging what's been lost.

Grief is God's invitation to honour the past while preparing for the future.

3. Stripping Away of Certainty

The ending phase often challenges the mental frameworks and theological assumptions you previously held.

- What it feels like: "I thought I knew what God was doing, but now everything feels unclear."
- What's happening spiritually: God is loosening your grip on predictability. Certainty is being replaced with trust. This is where faith becomes real-not in outcomes, but in relationship.
- Biblical parallel: Job losing everything and yet declaring, "Though He slay me, yet will I trust Him" (Job 13:15).

Certainty is not a prerequisite for obedience-faith is.

4. Questions of Worth and Calling

Without the affirmation of roles, titles, or outcomes, leaders often begin to question their purpose or significance.

- What it feels like: "Was any of it worth it?" "Am I still called?" "What do I do now?" 'Did I fail God?'
- What's happening spiritually: God is purifying your motives. He's inviting you to trust that your worth isn't based on visible fruit, but on being His beloved.
- Reframing: The loss of people, change of role or change is not the loss of calling-it may be the deepening of it.

In this phase, God doesn't revoke your calling-He refines it.

Practical Tips for Navigating Endings

Endings are sacred. They are often uncomfortable, but they can become powerful catalysts for growth and intimacy with God when stewarded well. Here are key practices for navigating this phase with wisdom and spiritual resilience:

1. Grieve Well

"*Blessed are those who mourn, for they shall be comforted.*" - Matthew 5:4

- What it means: Don't rush past your emotional response. Grief is not a detour from faith-it is a pathway into deeper trust.
- How to do it: Give yourself permission to cry, mourn, or feel disappointment. Journal your thoughts, pray raw prayers (like David did in the Psalms), and don't isolate yourself. Grieving in safe community is powerful.

- Why it matters: Unprocessed grief can lead to bitterness, cynicism, or emotional numbness.

Grieving well creates space for healing and honest reflection.

2. Name the Loss

"*The truth will set you free.*" - John 8:32

- What it means: Be honest about what has ended- whether it's a role, a relationship, a dream, or a season of influence, money etc.
- How to do it: Say it aloud to God, a mentor, or write it down: "This part of my life is over, and it hurts." Naming the loss gives language to what you're experiencing and opens the door to healing.
- Why it matters: Denial keeps you stuck. Clarity leads to forward movement.

3. Practice Surrender

"*Not my will, but Yours be done.*" - Luke 22:42

- What it means: Let go of needing to control outcomes, timelines, or how others perceive your transition.
- How to do it: Regularly pray prayers of surrender. For example: "God, I release the need to understand. I trust You are still leading me."
- Why it matters: Surrender invites the peace of God into the chaos of uncertainty. It also allows space for the Holy Spirit to guide rather than striving or anxiety.

4. Stay Rooted in Scripture

"*Your word is a lamp to my feet and a light to my path.*" - Psalm 119:105

- What it means: In times of transition, emotions can cloud discernment. God's Word anchors your identity, calling, and perspective.
- How to do it: Meditate on Scriptures of comfort, guidance, and identity. The Psalms are especially helpful-David gives permission to feel everything while still trusting God.
- Why it matters: Scripture reorients you to truth when life feels uncertain or when you feel unseen and unanchored.

5. Resist Premature Replacements

"*Be still before the Lord and wait patiently for him.*" - Psalm 37:7

- What it means: Don't rush to fill the void left by what's ended with something new just to avoid discomfort.
- How to do it: When tempted to jump into a new project, role, or relationship immediately, pause and ask: "Am I running from pain or responding to God?"
- Why it matters: False starts can delay true transition. Waiting may feel unproductive, but it's often where God is forming depth and clarity for the next step.

2. Liminal Space: Waiting, Transformation, and Hidden Work

Holy Saturday—the day between crucifixion and resurrection—is the liminal space of the Cross. It is a space of non-structure where Jesus' body lay in the tomb, and His followers were disoriented and afraid. A liminal period is a disorienting period of non-structure or anti-structure that opens new possibilities no longer based on old status or power hierarchies. New identities are explored, and new possibilities are considered. For leaders, liminal seasons might look like:

- Being in between assignments
- Waiting on God’s direction
- Navigating a season where vision is unclear
- Feeling spiritually dry or invisible
- Being misunderstood or overlooked

Characteristics of the Liminal Stage

The liminal stage is the “in-between” season—no longer where you were, but not yet where you’re going. It can feel deeply unsettling, but it is often the very place where God forms the inner life of a leader. Like Israel in the wilderness, Jesus in the desert, or Joseph in prison, this stage is less about activity and more about identity, intimacy, and formation.

1. Disidentification

"You're not who you were, but not yet who you're becoming."

- What it means: The title, status, or sense of self you once carried no longer applies. You feel unmoored or in limbo.
- How it manifests: You might feel like you're "between assignments" or unsure of your purpose. People may not know how to relate to you anymore, and you may not know how to relate to yourself.
- Spiritual significance: God is stripping away false identities so He can root you in your true identity as His child, not your role, productivity, or public image.

2. Isolation or Wilderness-Like Experiences

"*Jesus was led by the Spirit into the wilderness...*" – Matthew 4:1

- What it means: This season can feel lonely, relationships shift, affirmation dries up, and familiar rhythms disappear.
- How it manifests: You may experience a withdrawal from community, platforms, or influence. Even your connection with God may feel quieter or different.
- Spiritual significance: The wilderness is not abandonment—it's refinement. God often withdraws external noise to tune your ears to His voice alone.

3. Temptation to Quit or Compromise

"*If you are the Son of God...*" – Matthew 4:3

- What it means: In uncertainty, there's a strong pull to escape discomfort—by rushing ahead, going back, or settling for less.
- How it manifests: You may be tempted to grasp for old positions, relationships, lower your standards, or question God's timing and faithfulness.
- Spiritual significance: Temptation in transition is often an identity test. Will you compromise for comfort, or allow God to form you deeply?

4. Inner Transformation and Heart Work

"*God does not look at the things people look at. People look at the outward appearance, but the Lord looks at the heart.*" – 1 Samuel 16:7

- What it means: God shifts the focus from external fruit to internal formation. This season reveals what's really in your heart—your fears, desires, attachments, and motives.
- How it manifests: Hidden areas of pride, insecurity, comparison, or ambition may surface. You may feel exposed, but this is grace.
- Spiritual significance: God is not punishing you; He's preparing you. The deeper the calling, the deeper the heart work required to sustain it.

5. Questions About Calling and Future

"*Lord, what do You want me to do?*" – Acts 9:6

- What it means: Your sense of purpose or vision may feel blurred. The clarity you once had has faded, and uncertainty feels overwhelming.
- How it manifests: You may ask: Am I still called? Was that season a failure? Did I miss it? What's next?
- Spiritual significance: God uses these questions to draw you into dependence, recalibrate your purpose, and help you discern His next assignment—not just what's next, but who you are becoming.

Practical Tips for Navigating Liminal Space

The liminal space—the "in-between" where you're no longer who you were but not yet who you're becoming—is sacred and unsettling. It is the wilderness between endings and new beginnings. While disorienting, this stage holds the greatest potential for deep inner transformation, if you learn to walk through it with intentionality and faith.

1. Stay Connected to God

"*Even the darkness is not dark to You.*" – Psalm 139:12

- Why this matters: God often goes 'silent' in the liminal place, not because He's absent, but because He's forming you beyond surface-level clarity. Trust Him even when you can't trace Him.

How to apply:

- Prioritise presence over answers—sit with God even when He feels silent.
- Practice stillness, contemplative prayer, and spiritual journaling.
- Learn to recognise God's work in the dark—maturity is often hidden, not headline-worthy.

2. Find Mentors or Spiritual Leaders

"*In an abundance of counsellors there is safety.*" – Proverbs 11:14

- Why this matters: The liminal space can feel lonely, but you are not meant to navigate it alone. Others can help you discern the terrain you're walking through.

How to apply:

- Seek out someone who has walked through transitions with God—don't isolate.
- Be honest about your doubts, fears, and confusion.
- Invite feedback and spiritual perspective, especially when you feel stuck or tempted to quit.

3. Avoid Shortcuts

"*Let endurance have its full effect, so that you may be mature and complete...*" – James 1:4

- Why this matters: The temptation in liminality is to escape discomfort. But hurrying the process can short-circuit the very transformation God is after.

How to apply:

- Resist the urge to jump to the next opportunity just to feel secure.
- Trust God's timing, even when it feels slow or silent.
- Ask: "Am I trying to move on, or am I letting God move deeply in me?"

4. Reflect and Re-evaluate

"*Search me, O God, and know my heart...*" – Psalm 139:23

- Why this matters: Liminality invites a redefinition of calling, character, and identity. It's a time to ask what God is doing in you, not just what He's doing around you.

How to apply:

- Journal regularly about what God is surfacing in your heart.
- Take inventory of old patterns, beliefs, or idols being challenged.
- Ask reflective questions like:

- What is God developing in me that success never could?
- What parts of my identity are being refined or removed?

5. Serve in Hiddenness

"*Your Father who sees in secret will reward you.*" – Matthew 6:4

- Why this matters: Liminal space is not passive waiting—it's a proving ground of faithfulness. Serving in obscurity builds strength and sincerity.

How to apply:

- Don't underestimate the value of unseen obedience.
- Look for small ways to be faithful—at home, in your church, or with strangers.
- Embrace the season as a time to serve without applause, trusting God sees it all.

3. New Beginnings: Resurrection, Recommissioning, and Renewal

- The resurrection is more than a happy ending—it is a redefinition. Jesus didn't return to life as it was; He emerged with glorified purpose and power. Likewise, new beginnings for leaders might include:
- A new role, calling and greater authority
- A fresh vision for ministry, family or business
- A deeper relationship with God

- A restored relationship or renewed purpose
- Unexpected doors opening

Characteristics of the New Beginning

The New Beginning marks the end of the disorientation of the liminal season and the emergence into a fresh assignment or identity. It is a season filled with divine clarity, empowerment, and purpose, but also one that must be approached with humility and intentionality. This stage reveals the fruit of transformation, and how leaders carry it will shape their long-term impact and sustainability.

1. Clarity of Calling

In the fog of transition, God often refines the focus of our purpose.

- Explanation: After the ambiguity of endings and the disorientation of liminal space, clarity begins to emerge. Leaders start to recognise what God was forming in them, and how that preparation connects to their next season of influence or responsibility.
- Example: Like Moses returning to Egypt with a clarified mission or Paul emerging from the wilderness with a gospel mandate, new beginnings bring refined vision.
- Leadership Insight: Clarity doesn't mean ease, but it does mean confidence in why and for whom you are stepping into this next season.

2. Spirit-Empowered Confidence

The confidence that emerges is not self-generated but birthed from God's presence and process.

- Explanation: After being emptied of self-reliance in the liminal space, leaders begin to walk in a Spirit-dependent confidence. This boldness is not arrogance but a trust that God, who called and refined, now empowers.
- Example: David, after tending sheep and facing lions, confronts Goliath not with bravado but faith-filled confidence rooted in prior obedience.
- Leadership Insight: This kind of confidence sustains leaders through future opposition because it's rooted in proven intimacy and history with God.

3. Recommissioning and Sending

The new beginning is often marked by a fresh commissioning—a public or spiritual recognition of a new role or assignment.

- Explanation: Leaders often experience a form of sending or release into their next assignment. This can be through prophetic confirmation, leadership endorsement, or an internal conviction made manifest.
- Example: Jesus, after the wilderness (liminal space), returns in the power of the Spirit and begins His public ministry (Luke 4).
- Leadership Insight: Recommissioning affirms that transition was not wasted time—it was preparation for deeper alignment with divine purpose.

4. Gratitude and Humility

The weight of what you've survived and overcome produces deep gratitude and a posture of humility.

- Explanation: Leaders who have truly journeyed through the pain of endings and the purifying fire of liminal space emerge tender, not entitled. They carry a grace-saturated perspective on leadership.
- Example: Joseph, standing before his brothers in Egypt, acknowledges God's redemptive plan with tearful gratitude, not bitterness.
- Leadership Insight: Gratitude preserves spiritual vitality, and humility keeps your hands open for what God wants to do next.

5. Fresh Identity Shaped by Obedience, Not Achievement

You are no longer defined by what you produce, but by who you've become through your obedience.

- Explanation: After the stripping away of the old identity and the testing of character in the in-between, a leader's sense of self is no longer rooted in titles, success, or performance. It is rooted in love, obedience, and alignment with God's heart.
- Example: Jesus receives the affirmation "This is my beloved Son" before He does any public miracles or teachings. Identity precedes performance.
- Leadership Insight: Leaders who draw identity from obedience can lead with authenticity and resist the pressure to perform for approval.

Practical Tips for Navigating New Beginnings

The new beginning stage is often marked by joy, restoration, and open doors—but it also comes with the risk of losing sight of the lessons learned in the previous seasons. These practical tips will help you navigate this sacred phase with wisdom, humility, and purpose.

1. Stay Grounded

"*He brought me up out of a horrible pit... and set my feet upon a rock, establishing my steps.*" – Psalm 40:2

- Why this matters: Success can be deceptive. After a season of struggle or obscurity, promotion may tempt you to forget the quiet place where God formed you.

How to apply:

- Keep spiritual disciplines (prayer, solitude, Scripture) consistent.
- Maintain accountability relationships that remind you of your 'why'.
- Make space for God daily before reacting to opportunities or pressure.

2. Share Your Testimony

"*Let the redeemed of the Lord tell their story...*" – Psalm 107:2

- Why this matters: Your story isn't just about survival—it's a prophetic declaration of God's faithfulncss for others in transition.

How to apply:

- Be vulnerable about both pain and progress.
- Look for informal and formal settings (mentoring, small groups, writing) to tell your story.
- Frame your story not around your strength, but God's sufficiency.

3. Build Sustainable Rhythms

"*In returning and rest you shall be saved; in quietness and trust shall be your strength.*" – Isaiah 30:15

- Why this matters: New seasons bring new demands. If you don't build rhythms of rest and renewal, you'll repeat old burnout cycles.
- How to apply:
- Schedule sabbath rest and personal retreats.
- Set boundaries around work, ministry, and digital engagement.
- Practice saying no to good things so you can say yes to the best things.

4. Walk Humbly

"*He has shown you, O man, what is good... to walk humbly with your God.*" – Micah 6:8

- Why this matters: Elevation isn't a license for pride. It's an invitation to deeper dependence on God.

How to apply:

- Remain teachable and open to correction, even in success.
- Celebrate others' wins—resist the urge to compare.
- Let your fruit speak louder than your platform.

5. Disciple Others

"*Pass on what you heard... to reliable people who are also qualified to teach others.*" – 2 Timothy 2:2

- Why this matters: Transition wasn't just for your growth—it's now a tool to raise up others.
- How to apply:
- Look for emerging leaders who need encouragement, not just instruction.
- Share principles, not just stories—help them apply God's process.
- Be present, consistent, and prayerful in their journey.

My Story: Navigating Transition

As you've read throughout this book, my journey has followed a pattern of endings, liminal spaces, and new beginnings. Resigning and stepping into transition was one of the most painful, disorienting choices I've ever made. With other losses compounding the weight, some endings truly felt like death. There were days I had no words left, yet I knew the Word of God had to become my anchor—not my feelings. I prayed daily, sometimes for hours, sometimes all day. My routine drastically changed, but that became a sacred space. Without distractions, God finally had full access to place me on His surgical table. The problem had never been His willingness—it was some of my core beliefs that had been restricting His work. It reminded me of those action movies where the gunfight finally ends, and the character suddenly looks down to realise they've been hit multiple times—bleeding out without even knowing it. Spiritually, that was me: carrying wounds I hadn't noticed until the noise stopped and the stillness set in. It was disorienting because I have a blessed life, a loving family, and so much to be grateful for—so I resisted any idea of being a victim.

But I came to see that needing deep surgery wasn't weakness and wasn't a plea for sympathy—it was an invitation to healing. In that quiet season, the Holy Spirit began peeling back layers of infection: faulty core beliefs, guilt from over-functioning, and mindsets that were no longer sustainable. Through it all, God met me with profound love and divine affirmation—the kind that makes public approval irrelevant.

This wasn't a solo journey. I was carried by a village of grace:

- My mother was a powerhouse of intercession, prayer, and fasting—her lifelong support was foundational and undeniable. My brothers formed a fence around me with their love and consistency.

- Dr Ralph modelled godly masculinity and gave strong, truth-filled counsel that shaped parts of me I didn't even know needed shaping.

- Dr. Sharon spoke prophetically into my life and shifted my understanding and direction.

- Jerome and Adrian provided formative, life-giving sessions full of support, wisdom and counsel.
- My clothes circle of bothers and friends were sounding boards, safe places, pillars and prayer partners.

This was a group effort, deeply spiritual, but also relationally grounded.

Something shifted. I began to see in the Spirit with fresh clarity, and what had once felt heavy now became light and joyful. Then, unexpectedly, I received an invitation from the embassy of a nation I had long longed to visit—this time as part of a diplomatic delegation. It was the fulfilment of prophecies that my leaders spoke over me on different occasions, yet it came when my circumstances still looked contradictory. I knew in that moment that God was honouring the formation He had been working within me. The Holy Spirit whispered, *"It's time to weaponise your story."* I realised I was being entrusted with a deeper level of prophetic revelation and a renewed sense of commission. Pain had been replaced by joy. Memories once marked by hurt were now healed and free of their sting. All I could sense was abundant grace. God had not wasted a single part of my journey. He truly had brought me into a wealthy place—and He will do the same for you, if you are willing to walk through the transitions with Him.

Conclusion: Transition as Holy Formation

Transition is not simply a bridge between seasons—it is the furnace in which God refines leaders for lasting impact. The theology of transition, anchored in the cross, reveals that every ending is an invitation to death, every in-between space a place of deep transformation, and every new beginning a resurrection birthed in God's timing, not our striving. For leaders, the ability to steward transition well is not a side skill—it is essential. It determines whether a calling is sustained or squandered, whether leadership flows from striving or intimacy, and whether influence brings transformation or simply visibility. David's wilderness, Moses' exile, Joseph's pit, and even Jesus' tomb—all point to a God who forms His leaders in obscurity before revealing them in clarity. In a culture that idolises speed, visibility, and certainty, the leader shaped by God must learn to grieve well, suffer well, wait wisely, and begin again with humility. This sacred process does more than change your circumstances—it changes you. As you navigate your own transitions, may you resist the temptation to rush past the pain or bypass the process. Instead, embrace transition as a holy encounter with the God who leads you through death into life, through confusion into clarity, and through wilderness into promise. Transformation is not a detour from your calling—it is the road to sustaining and birthing it.

Chapter 13 Reflections: Theology of Transition

Memory Verse

'There is a time for everything, and a season for every activity under the heavens.' - Ecclesiastes 3:1

Personal Reflection Questions

The cross teaches us that God's pathway to resurrection always passes through death and burial. Likewise, every divine transition includes an ending, a liminal space, and a new beginning. These stages shape us deeply—if we allow them to.

1. Endings
    - What has come to an end in your life recently? (Job, relationship, identity, ministry role?)
    - Have you fully acknowledged the loss or are you avoiding it?
    - What emotions (grief, fear, confusion) have surfaced during this ending?
    - Are you trying to replace what's lost too quickly or are you surrendering it to God?
    - How can you invite God into your process of grief and letting go?
2. Liminal Space (The In-Between)
    - Do you feel disoriented or in-between identities right now?

- Where do you feel most uncertain or tempted to quit?
- What do you sense God is forming in you that success never could?
- Are you staying rooted in God's presence even when you don't feel His nearness?
- Who are the wise voices (mentors, spiritual directors) walking with you in this season?
- Are you tempted to rush this process or are you submitting to God's timing?
- How can you serve and remain faithful in hiddenness while you wait?

3. New Beginnings

- What new doors or opportunities is God opening for you?
- How are you staying grounded in the hidden lessons God taught you?
- Are you building rhythms that guard your heart from burnout or pride?
- Who are you called to share your story with so they can learn from your journey?
- How can you disciple others from a place of humility and gratitude?
- Are you walking in resurrection favour with a heart that points back to Jesus?

Closing Prayer

Father, You are the God of all transitions—of endings, wilderness, and new beginnings. Thank You for the cross that shows me how to surrender to Your process, even when it feels painful or unclear. Help me grieve well, wait patiently, and walk humbly into the new things You are doing. Refine me in the in-between and form Christ within me. May every step of this transition bring me deeper into intimacy with You and make me a more faithful, Spirit-led leader. In Jesus' name, Amen.

Chapter 14

The Kind of leaders God is Raising

The kind of leaders God is raising in this generation are those who operate from their prophetic identity—an identity revealed by God, rooted in His Word, and activated through surrender and obedience to The Holy Spirit. Unlike perceived or projected identities shaped by culture or personal experiences, prophetic identity empowers leaders to walk in divine authority and fulfil their God-ordained assignments. This chapter casts a prophetic vision of leadership by exploring how God activates prophetic identity and how emerging leaders can partner with Him to become effective vessels of His purpose.

In every generation, God raises up leaders who reflect His heart and execute His mission on the earth. To become one of these leaders, identity must be rightly understood and aligned with Heaven's perspective. There are at least three dimensions of identity:

- Perceived identity—who we believe we are based on past experiences, upbringing, trauma, or success.
- Projected identity—the version of ourselves we present to others, often shaped by societal expectations, roles, or desire for approval.
- Prophetic identity—the true identity assigned by God in Christ, revealed by the Holy Spirit, and grounded in Scripture.

Many remain bound by their perceived or projected identities, never stepping into the fullness of their calling. However, prophetic identity is what qualifies and positions a person to carry out the divine mandate on their life. To "activate" means to make something active or operative. God initiates the activation of our prophetic identity, but we must respond in faith and obedience.

The life of David provides a powerful model for understanding this process. Called from obscurity and anointed as king while still a boy, David's journey was marked by trials, transformation, and ultimately triumph. Through his life, we see the character traits, postures, and spiritual principles that mark the kind of leaders God is raising in this hour.

This chapter unpacks those truths by outlining seven key principles drawn from David's life—principles that will equip you to shed false identities, embrace your prophetic identity, and walk boldly in your God-ordained assignment

Principle 1: Those who Embrace Prophecy

"*And he sent and brought him in. Now he was ruddy and had beautiful eyes and was handsome. And the Lord said, 'Arise, anoint him, for this is he.' Then Samuel took the horn of oil and anointed him in the midst of his brothers. And the Spirit of the Lord rushed upon David from that day forward. And Samuel rose up and went to Ramah.*" —1 Samuel 16:12–13

Prophecy: Heaven's Perspective

The kind of leaders God is raising are those who embrace prophecy. Prophecy is God's counsel concerning who we are, what is coming, and how we are to walk into it. The Bible is the first and final authority for prophetic revelation—it is God's written prophecy to humanity.

Prophecy originates not on Earth but from the Throne of God. It travels through generations, locating those whose hearts are postured toward obedience. In Scripture, we often see prophetic words "land" in environments that seem completely contradictory. That's intentional—God often speaks His Word in the middle of contradiction. David was the youngest of his brothers yet chosen by God. Tradition said the eldest should receive this honour, but God bypassed tradition and perception to honour the heart. While David's brothers had the outward appearance of leadership, God was looking for a heart aligned with Heaven (1 Samuel 16:7).

Contradiction Isn't Disqualification

David was overlooked by his family, likely ridiculed and potentially shunned due to circumstances surrounding his birth (Psalm 51:5; 69:8). Despite this, God ensured the prophetic word found him in the fields. God bypassed familial and cultural structures to reach the one He had chosen. Your contradiction does not disqualify you. From Heaven's perspective, it may qualify you even more (1 Corinthians 1:27–31). God is not intimidated by your contradictions—He's glorified through them. Your family background, social status can't block God's call. What you think is a barrier is what God will use as a stage!

Anointed but Not Yet Appointed

David was anointed but remained in the same situation. The anointing represents empowerment by the Holy Spirit, but appointment speaks of being installed into your calling. Many people are anointed but remain unappointed because they don't faithfully walk through the process of preparation. Can you remain in obscurity and still steward the anointing well? David didn't promote himself or try to force the prophecy. He let the Word of the Lord shape his character and behaviour. He learned how to be a king before ever sitting on a throne. Everything Jesus did was to fulfil Scripture (Matthew 1:22, 4:12–16, 26:56). Like Jesus, we were born to fulfil a prophetic word. We must walk with situational awareness, constantly asking: How does this moment align with God's Word?

Don't Be a Saul

At the time David was anointed, Saul was still king. One had position without anointing, the other had anointing without position. What separated them? Obedience to God's prophetic word. Saul lost his place because he rejected the prophecy spoken over Israel (Exodus 17:14, 1 Samuel 15). God had given him a mission, but he chose compromise and reputation over obedience. A position does not make you a leader. Obedience does.

The Bible Is Your First Prophetic Word

Even if no prophet visits your house, you are not without prophecy. The Word of God declares your prophetic identity:

- You are chosen (1 Peter 2:9).
- You are His workmanship (Ephesians 2:10).
- You are more than a conqueror (Romans 8:37).

Don't underestimate the seeds the Word plants in you. David meditated on the prophecy and fought back with it – something Paul taught Timothy to do in the New Testament (1 Timothy 1:18). When his environment contradicted his destiny, the Word kept him aligned. The people around you, or even your own emotions, might be telling you something different from what God has said—but you must clothe your mind in Scripture and be prayerful. We don't just read the Bible to preach or fast for ministry engagements. We read and fast to transform our minds and step into our assignment.

Principle 2: Those Who Engage with Crisis

"*If he is able to fight with me and kill me, then we will be your servants. But if I prevail against him and kill him, then you shall be our servants and serve us." And the Philistine said, "I defy the ranks of Israel this day. Give me a man, that we may fight together." When Saul and all Israel heard these words of the Philistine, they were dismayed and greatly afraid.*" —1 Samuel 17:9–11

Crisis Is a Catalyst for Leadership

The kind of leaders God is raising are those who do not run from crisis but engage with it. A crisis is a time of intense difficulty, danger, or a pivotal moment when a crucial decision must be made. These moments often serve as divine platforms for leadership to emerge. David didn't need to manufacture an opportunity for promotion. He didn't force his way into visibility. God used a national crisis—Goliath—to position David for his appointed calling. Goliath was not David's obstacle; he was David's platform.

Let this speak to you: You don't need to scheme to be seen! You don't have to manipulate or orchestrate moments of elevation. If God has truly called you, He will use even the loudest enemy threats as the stage for your emergence.

Pure Motives Matter

David trusted God enough to wait. He wasn't trying to overthrow Saul or seek glory through rebellion. Some leaders today may feel they are called, yet their hearts are compromised by fear, insecurity, or selfish ambition. The means to your calling must be as pure as the end. If you manipulate your way to the 'top', you'll have to keep manipulating to stay there. David's emergence came through serving, not striving. He was simply delivering food to his brothers, when he heard Goliath's defiant taunts. That moment triggered the anointing within him. Crisis didn't intimidate David—it activated him. The anointing is activated by problems.

Crisis Reveals Character

This particular crisis revealed the limitations of Saul's leadership and the spiritual condition of Israel. Goliath exposed the absence of courage, faith, and prophetic vision in the current leadership. Saul had the position, but not the power. David had the power, even before having the position. Crisis is not just circumstantial—it is revelatory. It exposes what's really inside of us. Who you are under pressure is who you are. God uses moments of difficulty to reveal, refine, and raise up leaders. The name "Goliath" comes from the Hebrew root word 'galah', meaning "to reveal, exile, or expose." God used Goliath to expose not only Saul's fears but also David's faith. In the same way, the crisis you're facing may be less about the problem itself and more about what God wants to reveal about you.

Crisis Is Generational

Goliath's origin traces back to unfinished battles in the time of Joshua (Judges 1, Deuteronomy 1:21). Israel had failed to fully obey God's command to drive out certain enemies and had compromised by making treaties. As a result, what one generation refused to conquer, became a crisis for the next. Let this sober truth sink in: One generation's compromise can become another generation's crisis. What giants are you refusing to face that may rise up in the lives of your children or community?

Crisis Produces Relevance

Your relevance in the Kingdom is often measured by your willingness to solve problems. Leaders are not remembered for comfort—they are remembered for what they built, broke through, or restored during moments of trial. During the global pandemic, some governments didn't see the church as essential because the church had lost its problem-solving power. But God is raising a remnant—men and women like David—who will rise up in their sphere of influence with wisdom, strategy, and power. What problems do you see in your family, church, workplace, or society? These are not just burdens to carry—they are opportunities entrusted to you by God. Your stewardship of problems will determine your relevance, the depth of your leadership, and the measure of anointing you will walk in. When you learn to see crisis through the lens of faith, you will no longer view it as an inconvenience but as an invitation from Heaven—a divine summons into greater leadership, responsibility, and purpose. Problems are often prophetic signals, pointing to where your voice, gifts, and obedience are needed most. God wants to use you as a solution in your family, your community, your workplace, and even in national systems. Your crisis is not just an interruption—it's an invitation.

Principle 3: Those that Serve Without Agenda

The kind of leaders God is raising in this generation are men and women who serve without personal agenda. How we steward our current season of service determines whether we are qualified for the next. Anointing does not automatically qualify us for leadership—character and faithful service do.

David's Journey: Serving in Hidden Seasons

David had at least three careers before ascending to kingship:

- The Shepherd (Stewardship)
- The Musician (Proximity)
- The Warrior/Armour Bearer (Preparation)

Although David was anointed as king by a prophet, he did not immediately step onto his throne. Instead, he went through seasons of testing, development, and faithful service. Training before reigning. Every prophetic word we receive must be followed by a process of preparation. Many want the platform, but few embrace the process.

Career 1: The Shepherd – Stewardship

"*But David went back and forth from Saul to feed his father's sheep at Bethlehem.*" — 1 Samuel 17:15

David didn't allow the oil of his anointing to make him abandon his father's sheep. He remained faithful to the task that seemed insignificant—serving at home. The test of stewardship is crucial in God's kingdom. Stewardship is "the responsible management of something entrusted to your care." In David's case, it was sheep. But in God's eyes, he was learning to pastor a nation. Many believers miss the extraordinary call because they fail to faithfully steward the ordinary. "Whoever is faithful in little will also be faithful in much." — Luke 16:10.

<u>Biblical Examples of Promotion Through Service</u>

- Rebekah (Genesis 24):

She wasn't discovered prophesying or campaigning—she was discovered serving. Her proactive kindness and hospitality led her to become part of the Messianic lineage.

She offered water to Eliezer and his camels. Rebekah's story shows that God notices those who serve in private. What you think is "just water" might be your divine setup.

- Ruth (Ruth 1-2):

She had every reason to leave Naomi but chose covenant over convenience. Ruth's loving faithfulness to Naomi ("Your God shall be my God"), her "chesed" (grace and kindness)—brought her to Boaz and into the lineage of Christ. What you sow as a follower, you will reap as a leader. Her story is proof that serving without an agenda leads to supernatural alignment.

The Garden and the Tabernacle: A Theology of Work

"*The Lord God took the man and put him in the garden of Eden to tend (avad) and keep it (Shamar).*" — Genesis 2:15

The Hebrew words "Avad" (to cultivate or tend) and "Shamar" (to guard or keep) are also used to describe Levitical priesthood in Numbers 3:7-8. David was unknowingly functioning in priestly training by shepherding his father's sheep – his 'secular' work. You can't expect God to give you your own if you haven't been faithful with what belongs to someone else. "Your servant has struck down both lions and bears… this Philistine will be like one of them." — 1 Samuel 17:36. David gained transferable skills through his faithful stewardship of sheep for his public confrontation of Goliath.

Career 2: The Musician – Proximity

"*And Saul loved him greatly, and he became his armour-bearer.*" — 1 Samuel 16:21

David didn't seek the throne; his skill and reputation brought him near it. He served Saul with integrity, even knowing the throne would eventually be his. This is the test of proximity—can you serve faithfully even when you know you've been called to more?

Proximity is a test of character. David passed it by refusing to attack or expose Saul, despite Saul's flaws and attacks. David understood the difference between intercession and accusation. Like Shem and Japheth (Genesis 9), he covered rather than exposed. Too many disqualify themselves in the proximity test by exposing their leaders instead of praying for them. For the sake of clarity: if a leader is doing something illegal it must be reported to authorities (Romans 13). When I say expose, I mean gossip or being overly critical of the leader. If you cannot honour flawed leadership, you're not ready for your own.

Career 3: The Warrior – Preparation

"*Your servant used to keep sheep... and when there came a lion or a bear...*" — 1 Samuel 17:34-35

David's preparation for Goliath didn't happen on a battlefield but in secret, with no audience. Private preparation produces public victory. We must not neglect the spiritual disciplines, skill development, and warfare training that happen when no one is watching.

God prepares His leaders in obscurity. If you can conquer lions and bears in the dark, you'll stand fearlessly before giants in the light.

Leaders Without Agenda

God is looking for leaders who serve because they love Him—not because they want a platform. Those who will serve with purity of heart, not to climb, manipulate, or self-promote. True leadership in the Kingdom begins with hidden service, humble beginnings, and a heart that seeks no recognition.

Ask yourself:

- Can I serve when it seems thankless?
- Can I honour flawed leaders while holding onto my promise?
- Can I prepare in private while others are promoted in public?

Time, trials, and truth will always reveal our motives. David's journey shows that the throne is never the starting point, but it is the reward of faithful service, tested character, and obedience without agenda.

Principle 4: Take Godly Mentors and Counsel

"*Where there is no guidance, a people fall, but in an abundance of counsellors there is safety.*" — Proverbs 11:14

Leadership is not a solo journey. God never intended for His people to walk without wise counsel. Every calling, no matter how anointed or gifted the individual, requires godly mentors and advisors to help guide, refine, and equip them for the journey ahead.

The Saul vs. David Dilemma: Mismatched Counsel

King Saul was an experienced military leader. Yet, in a moment of crisis, he tried to advise David on how to fight a battle that he himself was unwilling to face. "*Saul clothed David with his armour... but David said, 'I cannot go with these, for I have not tested them.'*" 1 Samuel 17:38-39. This presents a critical lesson: not all advice is equal—even if it comes from authority figures.

Ask yourself:

- How can someone advise me in a battle they are not prepared to fight?
- How can you counsel me without any spiritual, practical, or experiential credentials?
- Are they giving me methods or principles?

Principles vs. Methods

Principles are timeless, but methods are contextual. Saul tried to give David his method—his armour and strategy from a previous season. But David understood that his current battle required a different approach. He had tested his own weapons in private and knew what would work for him.

The kind of leaders God is raising today must discern the difference. We need mentors and advisors who:

- Transfer principles not outdated methods.
- Help interpret the voice of God in our current context.
- Walk with humility, experience, and accountability.

Surround Yourself with Multidimensional Counsel

To walk in your prophetic identity and calling, you need more than spiritual encouragement—you need wisdom in every area of life. The Bible doesn't only advocate for prophetic input but for a multitude of counsellors.

Consider:

- Spiritual Counsel – Pastors, prophets, and mature believers.

- Financial Counsel – A financial advisor who understands stewardship.

- Professional Counsel – Pay for quality advice; it's an investment, not a cost. "Of what use is money in the hand of a fool, since he has no desire to get wisdom?" Proverbs 17:16

- Community Counsel – Ask questions within your local church. Sometimes the wisdom you need is sitting next to you every Sunday. You will never grow beyond your willingness to seek and submit to wise instruction.

The Posture of a Learner

The best kind of leader is willing to learn. God doesn't waste oil on those who reject instruction. David's greatness wasn't just in his courage—it was in his discernment. He could honour Saul's position but rejected his misaligned advice. Some people carry titles but lack credibility in their calling. Respect them, but don't let them clothe you with strategies that aren't aligned with your assignment.

Principle 5: Those who Manage Opposition

"*Now Eliab, his eldest brother, heard when he spoke to the men. And Eliab's anger was kindled against David, and he said, 'Why have you come down? And with whom have you left those few sheep in the wilderness? I know your presumption and the evil of your heart, for you have come down to see the battle.*'" — 1 Samuel 17:28

One of the greatest tests in stepping into your prophetic identity is not just opposition from the outside—but opposition from the familiar. David wasn't attacked by Goliath first—he was opposed by his own brother, Eliab. And Eliab wasn't just any brother. He had been present at David's anointing, and perhaps what we see in his words is a subtle mix of envy, pride, and projection. Eliab was angry at David for stepping up when no one else—including himself—was willing to face the giant.

Criticism from the Sidelines

It's always easier to critique from the sidelines than to step into the ring.

When I used to play for a football team one thing was clear: some spectators shouting instructions from the stands often don't have the skill or courage to play the game themselves. In the same way, many will shout from a distance, offering unsolicited opinions, while refusing to confront their own "Goliaths." David's response to opposition reveals a key transition: He was no longer just a shepherd asking questions—he was beginning to think like a soldier and a leader. Eliab tried to drag him back to an old identity or season with a comment that sounded like: "Shouldn't you be back with the sheep?"

Don't Let Envy Define Your Assignment

Sometimes, the people closest to you will try to shrink your purpose to make themselves more comfortable. Have you ever felt like stepping into God's call stirred resistance not from strangers, but from those who think they know you best? Let this be clear: Other people's insecurities are not your instruction. David had to decide: Will I stay small to keep others comfortable, or will I rise to the level of my calling? It's worth noting that David was misjudged as proud when he was actually the most humble and obedient one on the battlefield.

You Can't Avoid Criticism

Some of us are so focused on trying to avoid criticism that we're paralysed from moving forward. The truth is: criticism is unavoidable. If you're committed to pleasing everyone, you'll end up shapeshifting like a chameleon, reinventing yourself to meet shifting public opinion. But people are fickle. People will praise you in the morning and question you by evening. You cannot serve God and public approval at the same time. Opposition is not always a sign you're doing something wrong—often, it's confirmation that you're doing something right. And more than that: Opposition reveals alignment. It will expose the people in your life who are for your position but not your purpose.

Hidden Callings Still Have Heaven's Attention

We must also learn humility by celebrating the callings of others—even when they look different from our own. Not every assignment will be public, but that doesn't make it less powerful. A hidden calling is not an invisible calling. Some are called to the battlefield, others to the prayer room. Some to the boardroom, others to the classroom. Heaven values them all. David's Response: "Is There Not a Cause?"

In verse 29, David asks his brother: "What have I done now? Was it not but a word?"

That word—"cause" or "word"—in the Hebrew is "dabar", which means purpose, assignment, or revelation. David wasn't driven by ego or ambition. He was driven by revelation. He knew that his presence on the battlefield wasn't a coincidence—it was part of his divine assignment. Let this be your anchor when opposition comes: "I'm not here because of ambition. I'm here because of a word."

Choose Heaven's Perspective Over Human Opinion

When people misunderstand you, question your motives, or try to reduce your purpose to something safe and familiar—choose Heaven's perspective. You were called for more than the applause or criticism of man. Like David, keep your heart pure, keep your focus clear, and don't get dragged into unnecessary battles with Eliabs. There's a Goliath waiting to fall—and your faithfulness to your cause will bring the victory.

Principle 6: The Power of Private Life

"*And Saul said to David, 'You are not able to go against this Philistine to fight with him, for you are but a youth, and he has been a man of war from his youth.' But David said to Saul, 'Your servant used to keep sheep for his father. And when there came a lion, or a bear, and took a lamb from the flock, I went after him and struck him and delivered it out of his mouth. And if he arose against me, I caught him by his beard and struck him and killed him.'*"— 1 Samuel 17:33–35

Before David ever faced Goliath in public, he had already conquered Goliaths in private—he just looked like lions and bears. This is one of the most overlooked principles of destiny: Public victories are the fruit of private preparation. Many people want to slay giants on platforms but haven't trained in the background.

Private Battles Prepare You for Public Platforms

David's confidence didn't come from blind arrogance—it came from private history with God. While others saw a shepherd boy, David saw a track record of God's faithfulness:

"The same God who delivered me from the paw of the lion and the paw of the bear will deliver me from the hand of this Philistine." (v. 37). David understood that it was never about Goliath—it was about the principles he had learned in his private life. He had already practised discernment, courage, conflict resolution, and responsibility in obscurity. The same God who gave him victory there would give him victory here. God doesn't waste your wilderness. He uses your private obedience to prepare you for public assignment.

Don't Waste Your Private Life

Too many of us waste our private seasons waiting for a "platform," not realising that the private place is God's classroom.

- David learned leadership by caring for sheep.
- He learned protection through fighting predators.
- He learned worship and intimacy by tending the flock with a harp in his hand and praise on his lips.

Everything God has for your future is connected to what you're stewarding right now.

If David had not tested his sling in private, he might have defaulted to Saul's armour in public—and lost the battle. God may bring the opportunity, but your preparation determines how you engage with it.

Cultivate Competency in Obscurity

Your private life is not invisible to God—it's essential training.

When preparation meets opportunity, it produces fruitfulness.

Ask yourself:

- How are you sharpening your tools in private?
- How are you building character when no one is watching?
- How are you practising faithfulness with the "few sheep" entrusted to you?

David used his sling because he had tested it. What are you testing now for the giants you'll face next?

From Burning Bush to Burning Mountain

Consider Moses. When he led Israel to the backside of the mountain, he wasn't exploring new territory—he was returning to the very place where he had first encountered God at the burning bush (Exodus 3). The private place became a public miracle. The burning bush became a burning mountain. God multiplies the future manifestation when you steward the present moment. What begins as a private encounter becomes a corporate breakthrough when you stay faithful.

Steward the Season You're In

Where God is leading you next is hidden in how you're preparing now.

If you skip the process, you forfeit the power. David's rise was not random—it was the result of consistent development behind the scenes. So don't despise the pasture. Don't overlook the lion. Don't waste your private battles. The giants you're meant to slay in public will fall because of your faithfulness in private.

Principle 7: Those who Act (Obedience)

"*But be doers of the word, and not hearers only, deceiving yourselves.*" — James 1:22

The kind of leaders God is raising in this generation are not just hearers—they are doers. They don't just receive prophetic words—they partner with them through obedient action.

Every Prophetic Word Requires Prophetic Work

David didn't sit idly after being anointed. He didn't wait for the crown to be handed to him—he went back to the pasture, then to the battlefield. He used the prophetic word as a foundation to build his mindset. The prophecy didn't make David passive; it made him proactive. When Goliath showed up, David didn't flinch. Why? Because his actions had already been aligned with his assignment.

Obedience Activates Destiny

David served faithfully, expected opposition, followed wise counsel, and then—when the time came—he moved. He didn't overthink it. He didn't delay in fear or pride. He took decisive action. Faith without works is dead. Prophecy without obedience is unfulfilled potential. Some of us are waiting for "the perfect moment," but David teaches us: The right time is when God opens the door and you've been prepared.

Your Obedience Unlocks Victory for Others

When David acted, Israel became conquerors through him. His courage gave them confidence. His obedience became their breakthrough. Likewise, there are people attached to your obedience. There are lives waiting on your yes. Your courage can shift an entire community.

Jesus: The Greater David

David's victory was not just a military one—it was prophetic. He foreshadowed the victory of Jesus, our true and better David. Israel was paralysed in fear, unable to face Goliath.

We, too, were powerless to face the giants of sin, death, and Satan.

But Jesus stepped in—one man fighting on behalf of all. He acted. David was sent by his father, so too was Jesus sent by His Father. He obeyed the Father—even to death on the cross. Through Jesus' obedience, we are more than conquerors (Romans 8:37). Through His action, we step into eternal victory. If David had not moved, Israel would have stayed stuck. What victory is waiting on your obedience? What breakthrough is on the other side of your action? Obedience is not just about faithfulness—it's about impact. So don't delay. Don't second-guess. The word has been spoken—now it's time to move!

Conclusion

David's journey reveals that divine purpose is fulfilled through a combination of preparation, obedience, and courage. He listened to God's voice, submitted to godly counsel, managed opposition with humility, and acted when the moment came. His private victories laid the foundation for public breakthrough. In the same way, God is raising leaders who will not just carry prophetic words but walk them out through a life of discipline and surrender. Your prophetic identity is not simply received—it is forged. It emerges as you partner with God to overcome trauma, endure testing, and submit to the hidden, often painful processes that shape character and calling. Every battle, every delay, every private moment of faithfulness contributes to your readiness. Your obedience doesn't just position you for personal victory—it unlocks breakthrough for those connected to your assignment. Step into the process, stay faithful in obscurity, and when the time comes, act. This is how prophetic identity becomes prophetic impact and prophetic fulfilment.

Chapter 14 Reflections: The Kind of Leaders God is Raising

Memory Verse:

"The Lord who rescued me from the paw of the lion and the paw of the bear will rescue me from the hand of this Philistine." — 1 Samuel 17:37

Personal Reflection Questions:

1. Obedience & Service:

    - Am I willing to serve in hidden places before stepping into public impact?
    - How do I respond when asked to do something that seems beneath my potential or gifting?

2. Responding to Crisis:

    - Do I shrink in fear or rise in faith when faced with overwhelming challenges?
    - Have I been faithful in preparing myself spiritually, mentally, and emotionally for my current season?

3. Mentorship & Counsel:

    - Who are the godly mentors in my life?
    - Am I seeking advice from people who are spiritually credible and aligned with where God is calling me?

Conclusion: A Final Word for the Journey

As you come to the end of this book, I want to thank you—for reading, reflecting, and allowing the Holy Spirit to speak to your heart. These pages have not been theory or distant commentary; they've been a window into the real-life formation of a leader—shaped by grace, fire, failure, achievement and the relentless mercy of God. I am a living testimony of the very principles I've shared. Not because I've mastered them all, but because I've been humbled, refined, and transformed by them. What you've read wasn't polished in a classroom or curated in a vacuum—it was lived out in the secret place, in messy conversations, difficult situations, in broken seasons, and in moments where only God could put the pieces back together. I've watched these truths not only reshape my life but ignite transformation in countless others—pastors, emerging leaders, marriages, and everyday believers who dared to believe God could still use them. I've seen discouraged hearts revived, callings reawakened, and leaders restored—not through hype, but through the power of the Spirit. This isn't just a leadership manual. It's a prophetic invitation to return to the feet of Jesus, to lead from wholeness, to surrender again, and to carry His presence with fear and trembling—and with joy. This is about *becoming* the kind of leader Heaven trusts. As I write this the Lord is showing me a picture of a woman being clothed in royal clothes. God is 'mantling' those He is sending and preparing to send in this hour. I believe God is raising up a remnant of leaders who will not bow to the crowd, compromise their calling, or sell their birthright for applause. Leaders marked by fire. Anchored in truth. Led by the Spirit. Formed by the Gospel. Driven by love. Walking in power. So, whether you feel on fire or barely holding on, I want you to know: God is not finished with you! Your past doesn't disqualify you—your willingness to be transformed qualifies you. Holiness is still possible and available in Christ. Wholeness is still possible. And Spirit-empowered leadership is still the plan. Let this book not just be information you consumed—but a catalyst for change. Let it drive you to prayer, fasting, to accountability, to Scripture, and into deeper intimacy with Jesus. May you become a living letter—read by all—of the redemptive, refining, resurrection power of God at work through surrendered leadership.

Now go—lead well, love deeply, live holy, and finish strong. Your journey, like mine, is far from over. Yes, it's the end of this book but the beginning of your season to lead from wholeness and live in His presence. You will step into your place of abundance in Jesus' name (Psalm 66:10).

With grace and truth,

Emmanuel

Appendix 1

Family Genogram Template

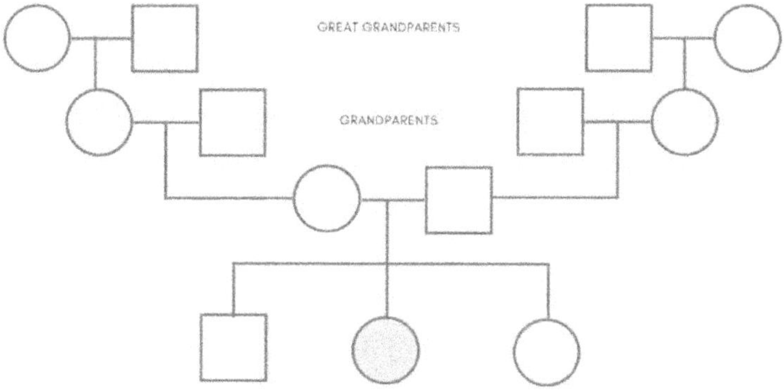

Simple Symbols Key

Symbol	Meaning
• Square	• Male
• Circle	• Female
• Blue	• Spiritually supportive
• Red	• Emotionally safe / trustworthy
• Brown	• Emotionally distant / disconnected
• X	• Broken or estranged relationship
• S	• Strong spiritual influence
• D/T	• Divorce or trauma
• U	• Unhealthy or dependent connection
• H	• Person who helped you heal

Genogram Questionnaire: You Are Not Alone

This questionnaire is designed to help you reflect on your family history, relational patterns, and spiritual inheritance. It is a tool for healing and insight—not blame. Use it to create a visual genogram and uncover any generational influences on your sense of connection, belonging, or isolation.

Section 1: Family Structure & Basic Information

1. List your parents, siblings, grandparents, and children (if applicable). Include:
   - Full name
   - Date of birth (and date of death, if applicable)
   - Marital status
   - Any notable life events (e.g., divorce, death, immigration)
2. Were there any absent family members (due to death, estrangement, incarceration, or abandonment)?

Section 2: Emotional Patterns and Relationships

3. Describe the emotional climate in your home growing up (e.g., warm, distant, volatile, peaceful).
4. Were there family members who were emotionally unavailable? Who were your primary emotional supports?

5. Was vulnerability welcomed or discouraged in your family?

6. Were you ever made to feel like your emotions were "too much" or invalid?

7. How did your parents or caregivers cope with stress or emotional pain?

Section 3: Loneliness and Isolation

8. Are there family members (parents, grandparents, siblings) who struggled with loneliness, depression, or isolation?

9. Can you identify any patterns of abandonment (physical, emotional, or spiritual) in your family line?

10. Were there times when you felt emotionally or spiritually alone, even if surrounded by people?

11. Were there secrets in the family that contributed to silence or disconnection?

Section 4: Coping and Survival Mechanisms

12. What common coping strategies did your family members use (e.g., silence, addiction, religion, achievement, humour)?

13. Has emotional suppression been modelled or normalised in your family?

14. What behaviours were used to avoid dealing with pain or conflict?

15. Are there any generational patterns of addiction, avoidance, or self-reliance?

Section 5: Faith, Healing, and Spiritual Legacy

16. Was faith or God talked about in your home growing up? If so, how?

17. Who was the spiritual anchor (if any) in your family?

18. Were there any unhealthy representations of God that may have contributed to feelings of abandonment or distance from Him?

19. Are there stories of deliverance, healing, or transformation in your family?

20. How has your understanding of God as a "present Father" evolved over time?

Reflection

- What generational patterns do you notice that contribute to isolation or disconnection?

- Where do you see God inviting you to break cycles and build new ones?

- Who has God sent (or is sending) to remind you that you are not alone?

Appendix 2

Circles of Intimacy Questionnaire for Christian Leaders

"Search me, O God, and know my heart..." – Psalm 139:23

This questionnaire is divided into four sections—one for each circle. Respond honestly. Use this as a time for self-assessment and prayerful alignment.

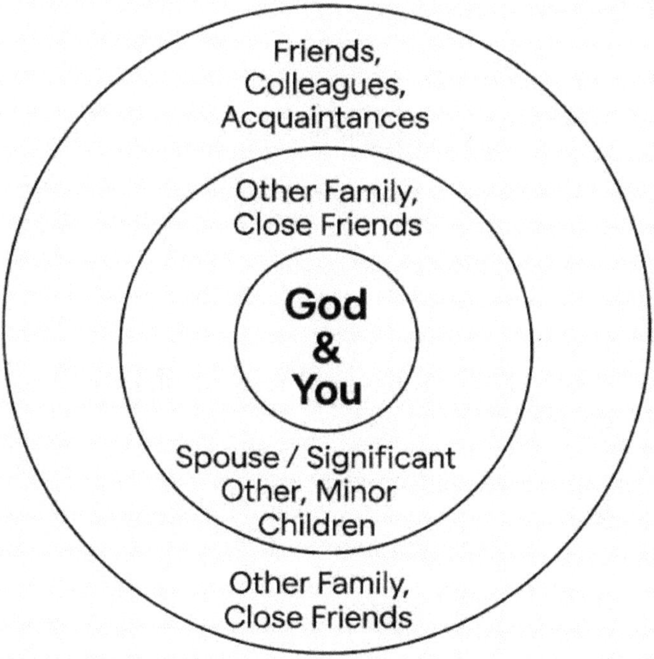

CIRCLE 1: GOD & YOU (Sacred Intimacy)

1. How consistent is my personal devotional life (time in Word, worship, and prayer)?

- ☐ Very consistent
- ☐ Somewhat consistent
- ☐ Rare or irregular
- ☐ Non-existent

2. Do I regularly reflect on my emotional health, thoughts, and spiritual growth?

- ☐ Yes, weekly
- ☐ Occasionally
- ☐ Only when in crisis
- ☐ Rarely or never

3. Do I prioritise physical rest, mental wellness, and soul-care as part of my calling?

- ☐ Yes, consistently
- ☐ Sometimes
- ☐ Not really
- ☐ I feel guilty resting

4. Have I placed anyone or anything (ministry, people, performance) in this sacred circle that belongs to God and me alone?

- ☐ No
- ☐ Maybe, unsure
- ☐ Yes, and I need to change that

5. How would I describe my current intimacy with God?

(Write a few sentences)

Answer:

____

____

____

____

____

____

____

____

____

____

CIRCLE 2: COVENANT RELATIONSHIPS (Spouse, Minor Children)

6. If married: Do my spouse and I feel emotionally and spiritually connected?

- ☐ Yes, strongly
- ☐ Somewhat connected
- ☐ We're drifting
- ☐ Strained or distant
- ☐ Not applicable

7. If a parent: How present am I with my children—not just physically, but emotionally and spiritually?

- ☐ Very present and engaged
- ☐ Somewhat present
- ☐ Distracted or often absent
- ☐ I'm not sure

8. Have I unintentionally placed ministry responsibilities above my spouse or children?

- ☐ No
- ☐ Occasionally
- ☐ Often
- ☐ I'm convicted about this

9. How often do I share quality time (not ministry time) with those in this circle?

- ☐ Daily
- ☐ Weekly
- ☐ Rarely
- ☐ Not at all

10. What needs realignment in my closest human relationships?

Answer:

____

____

____

____

____

____

____

____

____

____

CIRCLE 3: TRUSTED FRIENDS & MENTORS (Spiritual/Emotional Support)

11. Do I have at least one or two safe, godly people I can be fully transparent with?

- ☐ Yes
- ☐ I think so
- ☐ Not really
- ☐ I feel alone

12. How frequently do I connect with people who pour into me (not just those I lead)?

- ☐ Weekly or more
- ☐ Monthly
- ☐ A few times a year
- ☐ Never

13. When I face emotional strain or temptation, do I have someone I can call without fear of judgement?

- ☐ Absolutely
- ☐ Unsure
- ☐ Not really
- ☐ No

14. Have I been overly dependent on my spouse or team to meet needs this circle should meet?

- ☐ No
- ☐ Possibly
- ☐ Yes, and I need to shift

15. Who in this circle do I need to reconnect with or intentionally invest in?

Answer:

____

____

____

____

____

____

____

____

____

____

____

CIRCLE 4: CONGREGATION, COLLEAGUES & COMMUNITY (Public Influence)

16. Do I keep healthy boundaries between personal life and ministry?

- ☐ Yes, very clearly
- ☐ Mostly
- ☐ Not really
- ☐ What boundaries?

17. Have I ever overshared with my church or mentees out of loneliness or a need for validation?

- ☐ No
- ☐ Once or twice
- ☐ Yes, often
- ☐ I'm not sure

18. Do I feel pressure to meet unrealistic expectations from people in this circle?

- ☐ No
- ☐ Occasionally
- ☐ Often
- ☐ Constantly

19. Do I find myself emotionally impacted (positively or negatively) by people too far out in my circles?

- ☐ Rarely
- ☐ Sometimes
- ☐ Often
- ☐ Always

20. What's one boundary I need to put in place or revisit in this circle?

Answer:

____

____

____

____

____

____

____

____

____

____

REFLECTION & ACTION

1. Which circle feels the healthiest right now?

- ☐ Circle 1
- ☐ Circle 2
- ☐ Circle 3
- ☐ Circle 4

2. Which circle is most in need of healing or realignment?

- ☐ Circle 1
- ☐ Circle 2
- ☐ Circle 3
- ☐ Circle 4

3. What is God saying to you right now through this exercise?

Answer:

____

____

____

____

Notes

- Beaumont, S., 2019. *How to lead when you don't know where you're going: leading in a liminal season..* Lanham: Rowman & Littlefield Publishing Group, Inc.

- Daniels, D., 2020. *Relational Intelegience:.* Grand Rapids: Zondervan.

- Earle Jr., R. H. & Laaser, M. R., 2002. *The Pornogrphy Trap; Setting Pastors and Laypersons Free from Sexual Addiction.* Kansas City: Beacon Hill Press.

- Goheen, M., 2014. *Introducing Christian Mission Today: Scripture, History and Issues..* s.l.:Downers Grove: IVP Academic.

- Laaser, M., 1996. *Faithful and True : Sexual Integrity in a fallen world.* Grand Rapids: Zondervan.

- Leadership Tribe, 2025. *Leadershiptribe.* [Online] Available at: https://leadershiptribe.co.uk/blog/the-drama-triangle-explained [Accessed March January 2025].

- Rosenberg, M. B., 2015. *Nonviolent communication: A language of Life.* 3rd Edition ed. Encinitas: Puddle Dancer Press.

- Scazzero, P., 2015. The Emotionally Healthy Leader. Grand Rapids: Zondervan.

- Wright, C. J., 2010. The Misison of Gods People; A biblical theology of church's mission. Grand Rapids: Zondervan.

Acknowledgements

As I bring this book to a close, my heart is full of gratitude. This journey has been deeply personal, and I could not have walked it alone.

To my family— No words will ever be enough to express the love and gratitude I have for my mother. My appreciation for everything you have done for me and taught me is inexpressible. Every soul that is touch through this book; my life and ministry must be added to your account in heaven. Thank you to my brothers for being a constant source of love, strength, and grounding. Your prayers, support, and presence have meant more than words can express.

To my friends who stood by me in quiet seasons and celebrated with me in joyful ones—thank you for your encouragement, accountability, and genuine care. I have true brothers and sisters in the faith who have become family.

To my spiritual leaders— Dr Sharon Stone, thank you for pouring into me, teaching me sacred truths through your example and ministry. I am walking in prophecies you have declared over me way in advance, and I'm truly grateful for your life. Dr Ralph Dartey, you are truly a pattern of godly manhood that has deeply impacted me as a man and leader. You prophesied four things that all have come to pass in an undeniable way. You are a true father in the faith.

To my therapists —thank you for helping me unpack pain, embrace healing, and find language for my inner world. Your role in my wholeness has been a divine gift.

And above all, to Yahweh—My Lord and saviour Jesus Christ - the Author and Finisher of my faith. All the glory belongs to You. You carried me through wildernesses at times I didn't think I could survive, and You graced me to lead, love, and live again. May every word in this book point back to Your faithfulness.

This book is a testimony of Your grace—and I offer it back to You.

With deepest thanks,

Emmanuel Adeseko

About the Author

Emmanuel Adeseko is a bold prophetic voice and transformational leader called to restore identity, release purpose, and build capacity in emerging and established leaders. A recognised apostolic teacher, Emmanuel is known for his uncompromising commitment to sound doctrine, prophetic clarity, and Kingdom impact across the UK and beyond. He leads and oversees a portfolio of initiatives that reflect both spiritual impact and societal relevance. These include the Lions Network—a leadership and equipping movement shaping influencers in both church and culture—Excel Midlands Ltd, a Birmingham-based social housing provider for vulnerable adults, and a range of mentoring and entrepreneurial projects designed to empower next-generation leaders. With two seasons of teaching on TBN UK, Emmanuel's message has reached national and global audiences. Whether in the pulpit, boardroom, or community, he carries a timely mandate to multiply leaders, awaken destiny, and advance Kingdom culture with power, presence, and precision.

Testify & Connect

For invitations and enquiries, email:
info@EmmanuelAdeseko.com

For free resources, courses, mentoring and more books visit: www.emmanueladeseko.com

Scan the QR code below to share your story or connect with Emmanuel Adeseko.

@EMMANUEL_ADESEKO